The SAINTS at the CHAPEL

Thrilling Tales of History's Holiest Heroes

Lambing Press

Copyright © 2017 Christopher Reibold

Published in the United States by Lambing Press.

www.LambingPress.com

ISBN 978-0-9978215-2-9

Book design by Christina Aquilina

Illustrations from *The Lives of the Saints*

by Rev. S. Baring-Gould (1898)

The SAINTS at the CHAPEL

Thrilling Tales of History's Holiest Heroes

by Christopher Reibold
"The Saint Story Guy"

Foreword by Mike Aquilina

Lambing Press | **Pittsburgh**

TABLE OF CONTENTS

ACKNOWLEDGMENTS

I want to gratefully acknowledge the support I have received for my writing, and storytelling from; my family (Mom, Laura, Jim, Rob, and Shealy), Mike Aquilina, Rebecca Pettigrew, Paul Binotto, Jim Hanna, St. Louise de Marillac Parish, WAOB Audio Theatre, and many others. I also want to particularly thank Most Holy Name of Jesus Parish, and St. Anthony's Chapel for their support of this project.

FOREWORD
By Mike Aquilina

St. Peter's Basilica in Rome is the largest church in the world and perhaps the most beautiful. It sprawls over acres and towers over the city's skyline. The artwork inside includes architectural details and sculpture that must appear on any short list of world masterpieces.

St. Peter's stands where it does — and as it does — for one reason, really: to give due honor to God for the work he accomplished in the life of the man who is buried underneath the Basilica.

The largest church in the world is really nothing more than a reliquary to encase the bones of the Prince of the Apostles.

Among the thousands who visit St. Peter's every day are many nonbelievers, who are deeply affected by the church's beauty. But the Basilica "works" best for those who know about St. Peter and his friendship with Jesus — who have heard the stories of the Apostle's call, fall, repentance, and eventual martyrdom.

In the case of St. Peter, Christians everywhere hear the stories hundreds of times over the course of a lifetime. They're proclaimed at Sunday Mass from the Gospels and Acts of the Apostles. They're key moments in the plot in popular movies, from Jesus of Nazareth to The Passion of the Christ. They're staples in any good Bible study.

Peter receives due honor because he's so well loved. People

(like me) identify with him in his weakness and bluster and desire to avoid pain. Because Peter is known, he is loved. Because he is so well loved, his relics receive due honor.

On a hilltop neighborhood in Pittsburgh stands a chapel that is small, yet like St. Peter's in important ways. It is a pilgrim destination. It was built primarily to house the relics of the saints. St. Anthony's Chapel houses one of the largest collections of relics on earth. Not even in St. Peter's can pilgrims see so many skulls, femurs, and teeth on display.

The sight moves people deeply. But, again like St. Peter's, St. Anthony Chapel "works" best for those who know the story — who know about the lives of the saints and their friendship with Jesus.

Christopher Reibold wants us to make the most of our pilgrimage, not only to St. Anthony's, but through all our years on earth. He wants us to know the stories of the saints who have gone before us — not so that we'll be entertained for a moment, but so that we'll be inspired for a lifetime. He wants us, as God wants us, to be the saints who go before the future generations.

INTRODUCTION

Relics are the physical remains or personal effects of a saint. The Catholic practice of keeping relics is often misunderstood. This practice has its roots in ancient Jewish beliefs regarding the need for proper burial, and the ultimate resurrection of the body. For example, in the Book of Exodus, as the Israelites are preparing to flee from Egypt, Moses commands them to gather up the bones of Joseph for proper burial in the future, when the Israelites eventually enter into the Promised Land (Ex 13:19).

In the Bible, relics are also sacramentals, or physical objects that God uses as instruments of grace. In the Second Book of Kings, we read that a dead man was restored to life when he was touched by the bones of the Prophet Elisha (2 Kings 13:21). In the Acts of the Apostles, we read that people touched cloths to the Apostle Paul, then took them to the sick. When the cloths were touched to the sick, their illnesses were cured and the evil spirits left them (Acts 19:12).

In the early Christian church, the graves of martyrs were used as altars. In the Book of Revelation, the martyrs cry out from under the altar (Rev 6:9-11). This suggests that saying Mass over the bones of a martyr was already common practice by the time the Book of Revelation was written (around 90 A.D.).

There are other examples of the importance of relics to the early church. Consider St. Polycarp. St. Polycarp was a student of

11

the Apostle John and later served as Bishop of Smyrna, a Greek town in what is now Turkey. St. Polycarp was burned at the stake around the year 155 A.D. An account of his death, compiled from eyewitness testimony, was written a few years later. This account, known to us as *The Martyrdom of Polycarp*, tells us that after his death, the Christians took up Polycarp's bones, which they considered more precious than gold, and buried them in a place where they would later gather to pray (*The Martyrdom of Polycarp*, Ch. 18).

Catholics keep relics for four reasons. First, to venerate the people represented by the bones. To venerate someone simply means to give that person honor. It is not a form of worship. In Paul's Letter to the Romans, we are called to give honor to people to whom honor is due (Rom 13:7). Keeping relics is one way that Catholics seek to do this, just as in the secular world we erect statues and memorials to athletes and war heroes. Second, Catholics keep relics for the same reason that we keep photos and the personal effects of deceased loved ones: there are things that we want to remember, stories we want to make sure that we continue to tell. Third, Catholics keep relics as a way of expressing our belief in the ultimate resurrection of the body. Catholics believe that not just any body, but *the* body from which the relics have come, will ultimately be resurrected in a glorified state. Finally, Catholics keep relics because they are sacramentals that God sometimes uses as instruments of grace.

St. Anthony's Chapel in Pittsburgh houses the largest collection of relics in the world outside of Rome. The chapel was built between 1880 and 1883 by Father Suitbert Mollinger, a Belgian priest with a passionate interest in relics and a great devotion to St. Anthony of Padua. Father Mollinger came from a wealthy family.

He used his personal funds to construct the chapel as a place to house the relics he had collected.

European churches and monasteries were often looted during the wars of the 19th Century, particularly as nationalists fought to unify Germany and unify Italy. Many relics were destroyed, or disappeared onto the black market. By assembling his collection, Father Mollinger saved many relics that might otherwise have been lost.

St. Anthony's Chapel was dedicated on the Feast of St. Anthony, June 13, 1883. Father Mollinger died two days later. More relics have been added to the collection in the years since Father Mollinger's passing. Today, St. Anthony's Chapel houses relics from more than five thousand saints.

I write short stories, sketches, and vignettes that dramatize the lives and legends of the saints. These short pieces are written to entertain and to pique interest in these fascinating people. I am a contributing writer and reader for WAOB Audio Theatre, and I tell my stories live at Catholic parishes and schools. Some of these stories, or versions of them, have been previously recorded for WAOB Audio Theatre or told at my live events. Readers can listen to audio versions of some of my stories, as well as many fine stories by others, at the WAOB Audio Theatre website: http://waobaudiotheatre.org/.

The lives of the saints have furnished us with many pious legends, folktales, and traditions. In the following stories, sketches, and vignettes, I have kept to the traditional accounts while modernizing the language, adding descriptive elements, and fictionalizing dialogue. With a few exceptions noted in the text, I have limited myself to stories known from earlier, and presumably more historical, sources, but I leave the question of where history begins and ends to others. I make no scholarly claims; I simply tell the stories. I believe these old tales are worth retelling because they are entertaining, inform the imagination, and teach virtue. In these stories, we find many of the elements of Catholicism: Jesus Christ as Lord and Savior, the Blessed Virgin Mary, the sacraments, saintly intercession, redemptive suffering, and so on. The comments that follow each story are informational. Any errors are mine.

This collection is a kind of sampler, an example of what used to be called a legendary. These stories and sketches are tied together by the fact that St. Anthony's Chapel has at least one relic on display from each of the saints featured in this collection. With relics from five thousand saints on display, it is not possible to include a story about each one. I have chosen these particular saints because they are noteworthy, have interesting stories, and are representative of the chapel collection. They also speak to the great number and diversity of Catholic saints.

For purposes of planning a visit to St. Anthony's Chapel, it should be noted that the chapel has relics on display from many important saints not included in this collection: St. Patrick, St. Francis of Assisi, St. Clare of Assisi, St. John the Baptist, St. Peregrine, St. Luke, St. John of the Cross, St. Teresa of Avila, and many others. These saints are well known, and their stories have been expertly told elsewhere. A complete catalogue of the relics on display can be purchased online or at the chapel gift shop. It is called *Saints & Blesseds Whose Relics Are in St. Anthony's Chapel,* published by Most Holy Name of Jesus Parish.

It is my hope that this short book will entertain, inform, and help people to get more out of a visit to St. Anthony's Chapel. A

Introduction

portion of the sale proceeds from this book will be donated to St. Anthony's Chapel to help conserve and curate the wonderful collection of relics housed there.

Your Brother in Christ,
Christopher Reibold

St. Anthony of Padua

Inacio was a strong, burly man. His long, dark hair was a tangled mess that poked this way and that as it fought to escape from under his long wool cap. He never trimmed his gray-flecked mustache; and, remarkably, the rest of his face was always covered with exactly three days' worth of stubble, never more, never less. He tended to squint, a common practice among those who have spent long years at sea, and he was rather too fond of gold jewelry. He wore a heavy wool jacket and went barefoot in all seasons. He tended to be cynical and not much interested in philosophy or religion. Still, there was a basic goodness about him. He loved to laugh, and he got on well with his shipmates.

On this voyage, Inacio had been assigned to care for Anthony, the sickly young friar staying in the tiny cabin aft of the cargo hold. There was something about Anthony that fascinated Inacio. Perhaps he envied Anthony's complete and unwavering faith, or his continued good humor despite his illness, or maybe it was Anthony's rich, powerful voice, which could hold a man spellbound for hours on end. Whatever it was, Inacio often found himself thinking of Anthony, and he looked in on him more frequently than his duties required.

One afternoon several days into their journey, Inacio stepped into the cabin and spoke to Anthony. "You've lost weight you didn't have available to lose, young friar. I fear you will soon disappear altogether. How long have you been ill?"

"All winter," Anthony replied.

"And that is why you left Morocco?"

"Yes, *amigo*. I am returning to Coimbra," said Anthony.

"No, you are not," replied Inacio. "The storm is driving us farther and farther to the east. The ship is slowly taking on water. We need to make port."

"What port, then?" inquired Anthony.

"Hopefully Palermo."

"Sicily! Ah, Providence is strange, no?" Anthony said with a wry smile.

Inacio did not respond immediately. He folded his arms and looked at Anthony. Anthony was lying on a narrow wooden bench along the wall opposite the hatch. His face and hands looked strangely yellow by the light of the oil lamp swaying overhead. His hair and beard were greasy and overgrown, while his filthy habit moved loosely over his emaciated frame, but his dark brown eyes remained focused and alert.

The cabin had no windows. The air was stale and smelled foul.

Inacio cocked his head to listen. The storm seemed to be passing, but he could hear the steady drumming of rain on the deck overhead. The wind remained high, though it was no longer constant. Inacio knew that the crew needed to make use of those high winds if they were to have any chance of reaching Palermo, so he surmised that they were now trimmed for broad running, and he prayed that somehow, they would tack their way to port before the ship came apart.

The ship listed to starboard, but Inacio could feel it moving powerfully through the water, despite the persistent chop, and he nodded in satisfaction, as he judged that they might just make landfall after all.

Inacio returned his attention to Anthony. "We have maybe a couple of hours, no?" said Inacio. "Now would be a good time for you to pray, Man of God."

Anthony smiled. "It is always a good time to pray, *amigo*."

Inacio thoughtfully chewed his upper lip. Then he changed the subject. "You are a wonderworker, Anthony. Every day I bring you food, which you do not eat, and yet I must empty your bucket twice a day. Tell me, young friar, how have you come to be on my ship?"

Anthony laughed, then coughed hard until his eyes watered and his chest burned. It took him a minute or two to recover his breath. Then he propped himself up on one elbow and spoke to Inacio.

"Ah well, I suppose it will pass the time. I come originally from Lisbon, you know. For a time, I served as guestmaster at the Dominican friary in Coimbra. One day, a group of Franciscans arrived at our friary. They had come to Coimbra to establish a new house for their order. As guestmaster, it fell to me to see to their needs."

Inacio interrupted. "And you sought to join them?"

"Not right away, no." Anthony continued. "I was very attracted to their simple way of life, but I did not consider entering into their order until news arrived that five Franciscans had been martyred in Morocco. It was then that I knew what I had to do."

Inacio anticipated where the story was going. "You had to go to Morocco yourself."

"Just so!" replied Anthony. "I requested leave from the Dominicans to join the Franciscan order, so that I too could travel to

Morocco to preach to the Moors and someday become a martyr. Ah, but God had other plans! As soon as I arrived in Morocco, I fell ill. I have been unwell for more than three months now. My brothers were finally able to arrange passage for me on this ship so that I could return to our house in Coimbra . . . and now I find that I am on my way to Sicily!"

"A strange twist of fate," Inacio remarked.

"Not fate," replied Anthony. "Providence."

"Just as you say. Tell me, then, how did you come to be called Anthony? That is not a Portuguese name."

"No, Inacio, it is not. My parents named me Ferdinand. However, the Franciscans placed their house in Coimbra under the patronage of St. Anthony the Great, so when I entered into their order, it seemed good to me to take his name for myself to mark the beginning of my new life as a Franciscan."

"I see," said Inacio. "And what work does God have in mind for an ailing Franciscan in Sicily?"

"I am curious to find out!" replied Anthony.

Inacio heard someone cry out overhead. He said goodbye to Anthony, then hurried out of the cabin. He climbed the steep wooden steps to the top deck two at a time. As he emerged into the open air, he was struck in the face by hard rain and spray driven nearly sideways by the wind. The storm had picked up again, and the captain had called for all hands.

Two *marinheiros* hung precariously from the Jacob ladders. At the same moment, both men pointed off to the starboard fore. They began to shout. In response to their alarm, Inacio looked off into the distance, and there, just at the limit of his vision, he could see the coastline of Sicily peeking over the horizon. The Sicilian coast appeared as a dark silhouette against a leaden sky, and Inacio realized that they were going to make Sicily, but they were going to do it the hard way.

*　*　*

At the Franciscan house in Forli, Anthony found himself confronted by a young admirer, a Dominican novice named Giovanni.

"What happened after you were shipwrecked in Sicily?" asked Giovanni.

Anthony replied, "Ah, well, we were assisted by a number of locals, including a group of Franciscans."

"Why didn't you stay with them?" asked Giovanni.

"For a time I did, and in fact I finally regained my health while in their care, but I could not stay. They were not prepared to accept me on a permanent basis, and they were preparing to go to Messina for a meeting of the order. Representatives from most of the Franciscan houses were expected at the conference. Francis himself was going to be there, and I desperately hoped to meet him, so I resolved to go with the Sicilian brothers to Messina."

"The food, I expect," said Giovanni.

Anthony looked puzzled for moment. "The food? Ah, my health? Yes! Yes! Good wine, and olive oil for the Moroccan malady!" He said with a laugh.

"Still, you haven't told me how you came be here in Forli," continued Giovanni.

"Patience, my young friend," replied Anthony. He took a moment to compose himself, and then he spoke:

"I did attend the conference at Messina with my brother Franciscans. Francis was in declining health by that time, but the great man of Assisi did grant me a brief audience. He recommended me to the Italian houses, but only the house at Forli was willing to accept me on a permanent basis."

"And so you came to Forli," said Giovanni.

"And so I came to Forli," confirmed Anthony.

"You live here, in this cave?" asked Giovanni.

"Yes, yes," replied Anthony. "We are a small house. There are no extra rooms. When I arrived, this grotto was being used for storage. Father Gratian allowed me to clear it out to use as my cell. I am only a short walk from the other brothers, and yet it allows me a lot of time alone. I enjoy the solitude. It is good for prayer and contemplation. Yes, the grotto suits me well."

Giovanni looked around. The cave was small, and there were just a few personal effects. Beeswax candles gave off warm light and an inviting scent. From the entrance, Giovanni could look down the valley and just see the town of Forli in the distance. The sun was setting. A warm summer evening was giving way to a pleasant night. This little refuge would be cold in winter, but Giovanni had to agree with Anthony that, for the moment, there was something almost magical about this quiet little place. He turned again to Anthony and continued with his questions:

"Do you preach each day?" He asked.

"No," Anthony replied. "Today was the first time I have been asked to preach."

"The first time!" exclaimed Giovanni. "Then what is your role here, and how did you come to preach so magnificently today?"

Anthony though for a moment before responding. "I usually cook, and wash the dishes."

Giovanni was astonished. "Cook! Wash!" he cried.

"Yes," replied Anthony. "And I am happy to do it. My life here is simple. There is a rhythm to my day, and the concerns of the world are far away."

"What happened today?"

"As I understand it, there was some confusion regarding who was to preach at the installation Mass. Father Gratian assumed that you Dominicans would want one of your own to preach, as preaching is so central to your charism. At the same time, you Dominicans seem to have assumed that we would want to preach, as this is our house. No one prepared a homily."

"So Father Gratian asked you to say Mass for us?" inquired Giovanni.

"Yes," replied Anthony. "Though I am not sure why. He wasn't even sure I that I am a priest. I tried to change his mind, but once I confirmed his suspicion that I am a priest, he insisted that I be the one to preach."

"An inspired choice, I should say!" Giovanni added with reverence.

"Thank you, my young friend," replied Anthony.

"What do you think will happen now?" asked Giovanni.

"What the spirit wills," Anthony said with a smile. "What the spirit wills."

*   *   *

Anthony came to Rimini, a beautiful but infamous town known for its pagans and heretics. It was late one summer morning when he began to preach near the harbor.

"Friends, hear me! I bring you the Gospel of Christ Jesus!" he cried.

A crowd began to gather, but they were not receptive to Anthony's message. They jeered and booed the young friar. As he preached the crowd grew larger, louder, and more hostile.

Anthony stopped preaching. Then he paused, smiled, and, moved by the spirit, he addressed crowd.

"If you will not listen to me, then I shall preach to the fishes!" he declared.

His declaration was met with howls of laughter.

Then Anthony began to walk east along the north bank of the Marecchia river, past rows of tightly packed shops and houses, all with red tile roofs and pastel trim. Pansies, poppies, and peonies bloomed out of window boxes and basket planters as a pleasant breeze blew in from the ocean.

The crowd followed Anthony, continuing their taunts, but they were curious now. What did the young friar have in mind? What was he planning to do? A few excited children ran ahead of him, as more people came out of their houses and shops to see what was happening.

Anthony arrived at the wharf. Fishing boats bobbed at their moorings as sunlight flashed and danced across the waves in the harbor. The fishermen had sold the last of the day's catch. They were now busy stowing their lines, mending their nets, and readying their boats and gear to go out again after dark, but when they saw Anthony and the crowd following him, they stopped to watch. Anthony waited a moment for the crowd to close in around him. They joked, laughed, smiled, and waited anxiously for Anthony to make a fool of himself, but they could not see what Anthony could see. They could not see the angels.

Suddenly, there was movement in the water. The crowd looked away from Anthony to see that the shallow, crystal-clear water of the bay was so full of fish that it was no longer possible to see the bottom. The bay was now a living mass of fish! Countless thousands of fish swam so close together that a man could not fit his hand between them.Anthony stepped out onto a rock outcropping that formed part of a natural breakwater. With his back to the crowd, Anthony looked out over the harbor, raised his hands, and resumed his preaching.

"Fish of the sea, I bring you the Gospel of Christ Jesus!" he cried.

As he spoke these words, all of the fish leapt out of the water as one, and the people fell silent.

*   *   *

There was an old man named Guillard, who lived in Bourges when Anthony was assigned to the Franciscan house there. Guillard was short, with a bit of a paunch and rounded shoulders that gave him a slight but permanent stoop. He wore his wispy white hair long, in the fashion of the day, and he was quite wealthy, though he was not given to extravagant living.

Guillard was not a Christian. He was a landlord and moneylender who owned several properties and held mortgages on several more. Nevertheless, as Guillard went about the town to collect the rents, mortgage payments, and other debts owed to him, he would often stop to listen as Anthony preached in the public square. Guillard was moved by Anthony's preaching, and he found many of the young friar's arguments persuasive. Still, there was one idea in particular that he simply could not abide, one idea that prevented his conversion. Guillard could not bring himself to believe that Christ is really present in the Eucharist.

One day, as Anthony finished preaching and the crowd began to disperse, Guillard approached him and spoke. "Brother Anthony, can you demonstrate, by some visible proof, that Christ is truly present in the host? If so, then I will embrace your faith."

"What do you propose?" asked Anthony.

"I have a mule," Gulliard replied. "I will shut the mule up in my barn, without food, for three days. Then I will bring the mule here and offer it oats. At the same time, you will return with a consecrated host. If the hungry mule ignores the oats in order to adore its creator, then I will believe. Do you consent to this challenge, Brother Anthony?"

Anthony thought for a moment. He did not like the idea of putting God to the test, but he firmly believed in Christ's real presence, and he realized that this was an opportunity to convert not only Guillard, but also the many other doubters and skeptics who would surely come to see him fail. So, at the urging of the Spirit, he accepted Guillard's challenge.

"I accept. Return here to the square in three days with your hungry mule," Anthony replied.

Anthony went back to his cell, where he spent the next three days fasting and praying. On the day of the challenge he rose early and said Mass. After the prayer of consecration, he set aside a host. When the Mass was over, he placed the host in a monstrance, and set off on his way to the public square. As he walked a number of people fell in line behind him.

Anthony led his supporters through the narrow cobblestone streets, praying and singing as they went. It was a lovely spring morning. The day was pleasantly warm when the sun was shining, but still a little chilly when it disappeared behind a cloud. The procession of the faithful walked past houses and shops where merchants and tradesmen were getting ready to open for the day. On they went past produce stalls, curious children, and barking dogs until they came to the center of town.

Two restless camps soon formed on opposite sides of the public square. On one side, Anthony and his supporters. On the other side, a much larger assembly of atheists and heretics, who laughed and jeered and placed bets at long odds against Anthony.

Guillard led his mule into the square. As promised, he had kept the poor animal without food for three days. Then he produced a full bucket of oats, which he placed on the paving stones just a couple of steps in front of the mule. As he did so, Anthony raised the monstrance high for all to see.

"Come, friend mule, and bow down before your creator," Anthony called out lovingly to the hungry animal, and the mule walked on past its oats to stand before Anthony. Then it knelt down on its forelegs and bowed its head.

The crowd fell silent. Everyone except old Guillard, who clapped his hands and danced with joy. Then he ran across the square. With tears in his eyes he repeated over and over, "Oh, Brother Anthony! Oh, Brother Anthony!"

Many were converted that day, and old Guillard more than made good on his promise to embrace the faith. After he was received into the Church, he used his personal fortune to construct a magnificent basilica to commemorate the miracle of the mule.

St. Anthony of Padua

*   *   *

Three days of rain had finally given way to a beautiful spring day. Easter was fast approaching, and Rome was full of pilgrims. The faithful were camped out by the thousands around the fountains, and in the public gardens where the crocuses and tulips were already in bloom. The shopkeepers, street vendors, and pickpockets were all busy attending to the crowds. On market days, the stalls and carts were overflowing with bread, wine, fish, and spring vegetables for sale to the hungry visitors.

Anthony was in Rome as the official Franciscan representative to the Holy See. His Holiness Pope Gregory IX was a great admirer of the mendicant orders, and he had heard of Anthony's gift for preaching, so it was not altogether a surprise when he asked Anthony to give the homily at the consistory.

The bishops stood as two aides helped the pope to the cathedra. The pope was nearly ninety, but he was still sharp, energetic, and as affable and outgoing as ever. He smiled at the assembled bishops as everyone found a seat. There, surrounded by beautiful paintings and statues depicting scenes from lives of Christ and the saints, the elderly pope greeted the bishops and offered a quick opening prayer. Then he motioned for Anthony to come forward.

Anthony began to speak, "My dear Brothers in Christ . . . "

Everyone snapped to attention. His rich tenor voice was powerful, and his speech was almost musical. He was indeed a captivating speaker, but that was not what amazed the bishops. The bishops were amazed because they came from all over Christendom, yet each bishop understood Anthony in his own language.

They whispered to one another:

"Is he not a Spaniard?" asked one.

"No. Portuguese," said another.

"Again, the miracle of Pentecost!" exclaimed a third.

*   *   *

The lovely little town of Le Puy lies deep in the Loire River Valley. Here, a tiny chapel atop the Needle of St. Michael looks down on a sea of clay roof tiles and a warren of narrow cobblestone streets. The town square lies just below the great cathedral, where pilgrims gather to begin their long journey to Santiago de Compostela, and nearby, Our Lady keeps watch over the town from her own hilltop shrine.

For a time, Anthony was custodian of the Franciscan House here. The beauty and mild climate of Le Puy suited Anthony and kept him in good health. He drew large crowds when he preached, and he came to know and love the people of the valley.

Still, there was one man who did not care for Anthony.

Renzo was a prominent attorney. He was very wealthy, but not in the least charitable. He lived for himself, and devoted his time to worldly goods and pleasures. He had no time for religion.

From time to time, Anthony used to pass Renzo in the street. When the two men encountered one another, Anthony would always uncover his head, and bow to Renzo. This upset Renzo, who thought that Anthony was somehow mocking him. One day, as Anthony removed his hood and bowed, Renzo stopped to confront him.

"Now see here! I have never done you any disservice, yet every time you pass me in the street, you a take a moment to mock me! Arrogance and condescension do not suit you, friar! I have half a mind to run you through with my sword!"

Anthony calmly replied, "I meant no offense. I only wish to pay my respects to one who will become a great martyr for the faith."

"What nonsense is this!" exclaimed Renzo. "You know very well that I hold a low opinion of your ignorant superstitions!"

Anthony smiled. "Nevertheless, it has been revealed to me that you will become a martyr for the faith. I ask you to remember me during your passion."

Some years passed, and Renzo forgot about Anthony's strange prophecy, but Renzo did fall into the curious habit of praying silently throughout the day. This disturbed him greatly. He would catch himself reciting the prayers he had learned as a child, and he developed an unconscious devotion to the Blessed Virgin Mary. He tried and tried to put these thoughts out of mind, only to find that by the end of each day he had effectively prayed his way through the psalms, repeatedly recited the Lord's Prayer, and prayed for the Blessed Mother's intercession.

The Bishop of Le Puy organized a pilgrimage to the Holy Land. Renzo, moved by some impulse that even he did not understand, decided to accompany the bishop.

When the pilgrims arrived in the Holy Land, Renzo experienced a complete change of heart. Moved by the spirit, he began to preach to any who would listen. Soon, the Muslim authorities arrested him. For three days, he was subjected to the most horrible tortures. Then, as he lay dying in his cell, he remembered Anthony's prophecy, which he shared with his fellow prisoners. He died proclaiming that God had raised up a great prophet in holy Anthony.

*   *   *

Brother Donato was a young Franciscan novice, assigned to the Franciscan house in Bologna where Anthony was teaching at the time. One fall night, shortly after matins, Brother Donato walked away from the monastery and from the religious life. The air was cool and crisp. Along the roadside, wheat bundles spoke to the presence of reapers. The harvest was underway. It was dark, but Donato knew the road well.

Three hours later, he was well on his way to Ferrara, where there was a comfortable little inn, a warm fire, and a pretty girl. Brother Donato smiled to himself, laughed under his breath, and then looked into his linen bag.

"Here it is! Here it is! Ah, what was I thinking!" he said quietly to himself. "All the fasting, the praying, the lack of sleep . . . what is it for? What good does it do? It was that Anthony! He is a charismatic one, but deluded. They all are . . . wasting their lives. Well, I'll have no more of it!"

Inside the bag, Donato carried a psalter, but not just any psalter, *the* psalter. The psalter that he had stolen from his teacher, the great Anthony himself, and inside the psalter were all of the notes and commentary that Anthony relied upon when he preached. The psalter would fetch a fine price and give him enough money to make a start in world.

Brother Donato reached into a pocket and pulled out an apple. He polished the apple quickly against the cleanest part of his habit, took a big, self-satisfied bite, then stopped abruptly.

The vision was private, meant only for him, and it only lasted for a second or two, but it terrified him. He had to take a minute to compose himself. His heart was racing. He was shaking. His hands were wet with sweat, and he was out of breath.

Brother Donato threw away his apple, turned around, and headed back to the Franciscan house at Bologna.

It was nearing dawn when Brother Donato arrived back at the monastery. Anthony was waiting for him. As Brother Donato entered the house, he simply handed the psalter to Anthony.

"Just so! I've spent the night praying for the return of my psalter, and here it is!" said Anthony.

"I know," replied Brother Donato.

"Have you anything else to say to me?" asked Anthony.

Brother Donato looked at the floor as he spoke. "Yes, father. Please hear my confession, and I will want to seek readmittance to the order."

*   *   *

Anthony loved Padua, but in that lovely little town along the banks of the Bacchiglione, he faced different challenges than he had faced as an itinerant preacher. Throughout his travels, Anthony had aggressively confronted all of the popular heresies. In Padua, however, he confronted the worldliness, decadence, and vice born of rich living, and these evils proved more resistant to his preaching than the battle of ideas.

Anthony worked tirelessly in Padua, often preaching and hearing confessions until late in the evening.

Tiso Borghese was a nobleman who owned a large estate outside of Padua near Campo San Pietro. Tiso loved Anthony, and
he had great admiration for the Franciscan order. From time to
time, when Anthony grew frustrated or exhausted, his friend Tiso
would invite him to spend a few days with him at his country
house.

During one such visit, Tiso Borghese awoke late at night. He
noticed an inviting blue light spilling out from under the door of
Anthony's room. Curious, he looked in through the keyhole. What
he saw astounded him! The source of the strange light was a most
beautiful child, a young boy, whom Anthony was holding in his
arms. Anthony was speaking softly to the boy, and Tiso realized
that the boy could only be the Christ Child.

*   *   *

For three or four days, a young boy had followed Brother Luke
about, often spying on him discreetly. The boy was maybe ten or
twelve, and unremarkable aside from his obvious interest in the
aging friar. Finally, Brother Luke took it upon himself to speak to
the boy.

"Can I help you, son?" he said. "It seems that you have become
my shadow. Every time I turn around you are there."

The boy puffed up his chest and made his hands into fists.
With fake courage and a hint of defiance he said, "Yes, I wish to
know the truth."

"About what?" inquired Brother Luke.

"You were friends with Anthony, the famous preacher, no?"
the boy asked.

"Yes, I was," Brother Luke replied with calm indulgence.

"And you were present when he died?" the boy continued.

Brother Luke simply nodded.

"Well, I have heard a story, and I don't believe it. I want to know if it is true," said the boy.

"I see. What have you heard?" asked Brother Luke.

"My friends all say that Anthony died in a tree. They insist upon it, but I want to hear from you how he died," said the boy.

Brother Luke laughed out loud, and then, with a smile, he told the boy the following story:

"Anthony was friends with a man named Tiso, who owned a large estate outside of Padua, near the Campo San Pietro, that included many acres of woodland. Anthony loved to walk there, and deep in Don Tiso's woods, Anthony found a giant walnut tree, where many birds nested. Anthony loved Padua, but he had become quite famous. Everywhere he went, he was accompanied by large crowds. There were times when he wanted to be alone with God, so he would slip away to Don Tiso's estate, and climb up his favorite walnut tree to watch the birds and spend several hours praying.

"Brother Roger and I, we were his constant companions . . . and we worried about him, you know? Anthony was not that old, but he kept up a schedule that would exhaust anyone. He had grown quite thin. We spoke to Don Tiso. The next time we accompanied Anthony into the woods, we found that a little treehouse had been built for Anthony and a little shelter down below for Roger and me to wait for him. But when Anthony came down from his treehouse, he did not look well. He told Brother Roger and me that he had experienced a vision of his own imminent death, and that he wished

34

to die in his beloved Padua. We escorted him out of the woods, but by the time we found our way back to the road he was too weak to continue."

"What did you do then?" the boy asked with keen interest.

"We flagged down a passing ox-cart. The driver helped us load Anthony into the back. Roger sat with Anthony. I sat with the driver, and we all set off for Padua."

"But they say Anthony did not die in Padua," the boy interjected.

"No," said Brother Luke. "We made it as far as Arcella. Anthony lost consciousness. The Poor Clares have a house in Arcella. We stopped there. There are four priests assigned to the house. They say Mass and hear the sisters' confessions. The sisters found Anthony a bed, and one of the priests was summoned to administer the anointing of the sick. Just then, Anthony awoke. He had hoped to die among his brothers in Padua, but he was granted the grace to make a final confession. Then he was anointed with oil, and he began to quietly sing his favorite hymn."

"What was his favorite hymn?" asked the boy.

Brother Luke began to sing softly:

> *O gloriosa Domina*
> *Excelsa super sidera*
> *Qui te creavit provide...*

The boy interrupted, "That is how Anthony died?"

"That is how Anthony died," answered Brother Luke.

"Not in a tree?"

Brother Luke laughed. "No, he came down from the tree before he died."

*   *   *

Brother Goro went to answer the door. He opened it to find a very old man who was both smiling and weeping. Then the old man looked at Brother Goro and spoke.

"Please forgive me, young friar!" he said. "I have come to offer my thanks!"

"My name is Goro. I am, well . . . the doorkeeper. Whom do you wish to see?" asked Goro.

"Ah! I wish to thank the Franciscans! You are Franciscans here, no? Of course you are!" said the old man in an excited voice.

"Yes," replied Goro. "This is a Franciscan house, but I . . . perhaps you wish to speak to the abbot?"

"Please, young friar . . . indulge an old man . . . hear my story," came the response.

With as much enthusiasm as he could muster, Brother Goro invited the old man in and found him a chair. Then he called for two of his brothers.

Goro gestured toward the old man. "This is . . . "

"My name is Niccolo," the old man interjected.

"This is Niccolo," continued Goro. "He has a story he wishes to tell us."

"Just so good friars!" Niccolo began. "As you find me, I am nearly 90, and frail, but I did it! I did it!"

"Did what?" asked one of the friars.

"I completed my penance!" Niccolo replied.

The brothers exchanged puzzled looks as Niccolo continued.

"In my youth, I was strong and fearless. My friends and I formed a gang of thieves; we preyed mostly upon people foolish enough to travel the Marche alone. We lived only for the moment. We would rob someone, visit our favorite brothels, taverns, and gambling halls, then disappear into the hills to await the arrival of our next victim."

Hoping to bring the old man's story to a quick conclusion, one of the friars spoke, "And you've made a good confession, and completed your assigned penance. We're very happy for you Niccolo . . ."

"Patience, please!" continued Niccolo. "You see, Anthony came to preach at Rimini."

Suddenly the Franciscans were interested. "You heard Anthony when he preached at Rimini?" they asked.

"Yes," replied Niccolo. "Anthony was famous. He was attracting large crowds. So one day, my friends and I went to hear him preach . . . to see what all the fuss was about. I must say that I did not expect his preaching to affect us the way that it did. The square was crowded. I remember that it was hot. Anthony spoke for more than an hour. When he finished and the crowd began to disperse, we approached him. We confessed that we were a band of robbers."

One of the friars, with a good head for math, started to speak, "But that must have been . . . "

Niccolo finished the friar's thought. "That was sixty four years ago," he said, before continuing with his tale.

"Now Anthony was stern with us, but also pleased that we had been moved by his preaching, and he earnestly desired that we should reform ourselves. So he heard our confessions and assigned us our penances. He warned, however, that any of us who returned to our old ways would come to a bad end, and he was right!"

Niccolo was speaking to the friars, but he was only half present. He had disappeared into his memories. He paused, and then with a faraway look in his eyes he lowered his voice and said, "Meo was the first to go. Ah! You should have seen him in his prime . . . tall, blond, with glassy blue eyes . . . the ladies loved him! Was it lack of resolve? Desperation? I don't know, but one night, he chanced upon a wealthy merchant on the Via Fulmiceno. Apparently, he did not see the bodyguards trailing discretely behind his target. They put two arrows into his chest the instant he drew his knife . . . and the others, Lotto, Pace, Tomme . . . they all died on the gallows. Strozza! Now, he made good on his promise to Anthony, but he has been gone for many years now. I am the last . . . and today is a great day. You see, for my penance, Anthony directed me to make twelve pilgrimages to the Church of the Twelve Holy Apostles in Rome, and there to ask saints Philip and James to pray for my continued resolve. It has taken me all the years since to save the money and find the time to make twelve trips from the Marche to Rome, but at long last I have finally completed my penance. You see! You see! Such was the impact of Anthony's preaching on me, and, well, I want . . . I need . . . to tell someone! I thought my story might mean something to you who follow in the footsteps of Francis and Anthony. Thanks for making a little time for an old man who will now die happy!"

*   *   *

Sunrise was still an hour away, but Joao the fisherman was hard at work mending his nets. Today he would trawl for sardines.

The summer festivals were fast approaching, and in Lisbon a good catch of sardines could earn him enough to care for his family until the following spring.

The morning air was cool, but the temperature would soon climb rapidly as the sun made its way over the horizon. A short distance away, on a beach below a long line of rocky cliffs, Joao's wooden *lancha*[1] bobbed in the surf before the wide Atlantic. The water appeared dark at the moment, but Joao knew that it would soon be azure and emerald, with sparkling flashes of sunlight.

Joao felt rather than heard the rumble of water entering into the many nearby sea caves, and he realized that the tide was coming in. It was now time to put out to sea.

There were innumerable little inlet beaches along this stretch of the Portuguese coast. Many, like this one, were known only to the local fisherman, and Joao thought that they must be among the most beautiful places on earth.

Joao's life was simple, but happy. His son was still too young to fish. His wife was given to worry, but she loved him dearly, and Joao was profoundly grateful for both her and his son. He was affable and easy going, greeting everyone with a broad smile that tended to emerge abruptly from the tangled mess of his beard.

Joao loaded his nets. He put on his oilskin and gathered up his remaining tackle. He was just about to untie his *lancha* from its mooring stone when he looked up to see his friend Rui coming down the beach.

Rui normally fished from another small inlet a short distance to the south. As Rui approached, Joao could tell that something was very wrong. He waved, and called to his friend, "*Oi, Rui, como*

---

1   *Lanchas* are traditional Portuguese fishing boats.

vai? Why aren't you fishing today?"

Rui did not immediately respond. Rather, he drew nearer to Joao's boat. Then he took off his wool chapeu, the long, floppy hat that identified him as a man of the sea. Rui did not look up. He did not meet Joao's gaze. He had to take a moment a moment to compose himself, to find his courage. When he finally spoke, his voice was soft, and strained.

"Friend," he said. "I have suffered a terrible loss.""Tell me." Joao replied with great concern.

Then Rui told the following story:

"The day before yesterday, when the storm came, I lost my boat. I was just finishing my supper when I felt the wind kick up. I feared that my boat might break free from its mooring, so I raced down to the beach. I arrived at the landing as the storm hit in earnest. Through the wind and rain, I could just see my *lancha* as it drifted out to sea. There was nothing I could do, save to appeal to St. Anthony for my boat to be returned to me. Unfortunately, my prayer remains unanswered, and I must find a way to feed my family. So I have come here to appeal to you, to ask you to hire me on as your employee for a time."

Joao was moved by Rui's story, and he had great compassion for his friend, but listening to Rui's tale remind him of something he had heard the day before.

"*Uau*, Rui!" He exclaimed. "I think maybe St. Anthony has come to your aid!"

"What?" replied Rui.

Then Joao told the following story:

"Yesterday, I ran into the Almeida brothers. They were caught out in the storm. They told me that, while they were fighting their way back to shore, they heard a man singing. Apparently he had a beautiful voice and was singing a hymn of praise. His voice must have been powerful, for they swear they heard him clearly over the howl of the wind. Then, for just a second, they saw him. He wore a Franciscan habit, and he was skillfully piloting a *lancha* through the wind and waves. He was hard at the oars and paid no attention to them. A moment later, he was gone. I confess, I didn't really believe them, but now I wonder. I think maybe St. Anthony rescued your boat – no?"

Rui did not wait for further explanation. He ran down the beach to the next inlet. He had to make his way to the top of a high bluff before he could round a point and descend to the beach on the other side. When he made it back to the little cove where he normally stored his boat, he found it. Someone had drawn it well up onto the beach and turned it over to dry. His nets and tackle were neatly stacked to one side. The green and white paint was flaking off in places, but his *lancha* was otherwise none the worse for wear. His livelihood had been restored, and he took several minutes to thank St. Anthony for his assistance.

*   *   *

Dona Dante was distraught. She had not heard from her husband since his departure for Lima several months earlier. She had written several letters to him, but had received no reply. The money he had left for her to live on was nearly gone, and she now feared that something terrible must have happened to her beloved Antonio.

The stress was taking its toll. She had lost weight. She wasn't sleeping, and it showed. Strands of gray had crept into her long, dark hair, and the lines on her face made her look much older than she actually was.

Dona Dante knew that her husband had a special devotion to St. Anthony of Padua. One rainy morning, as she considered what to do, an idea came to her.

Senora Dante composed a letter to her husband. Then she worked her *peineta* into place, secured her black mantilla to it, and headed out into the cold Oveido morning.

Dark clouds rolled overhead. A storm was brewing. Now and again the wind would gust, causing spouts and shutters to clang and rumble against the sides of buildings.

A few drops of rain found her as hurried through the empty streets.

Soon she came to the Convent of St. Francis, where there was an old church used primarily by members of the order. She hurried inside, found the font, and dipped her fingers. The sanctuary lamp was lit, so she got down on both knees. With a slight bow, she made the sign of the cross.

Dona Dante looked around. She was alone. The church was beautiful, but she was not here to admire the stained-glass windows, or the paintings, or the racks of votive candles burning away in memory of the dead.

She found what she was looking for to the left of the altar. There stood a nearly life-sized wooden statue of St. Anthony of Padua, dressed in a woolen habit.

Dona Dante went to the statue and placed her letter in its outstretched hand. Then she took a seat in the front pew, composed herself, and offered the following prayer:

"St. Anthony, I beg your intercession. I have not heard from my husband Antonio since he left Spain to establish his business in Peru. I fear that something terrible has happened to him. St. Anthony, my husband has always had a special devotion to you. Please, guide my letter to him, and obtain for me a quick reply."

The next day, Dona Dante returned to the little Church of St. Francis, where she found her letter still in the hand of the statue as she had left it the day before, and she interpreted the failure of St. Anthony to intercede on her behalf to mean that her husband must have died.

She began to cry.

Now the sacristan happened to be in the church at the time. He heard Dona Dante crying, and he went to her. When the sacristan asked her what was wrong, she explained about her husband, his silence since leaving for Lima, and the letter that she had placed under St. Anthony's protection.

The sacristan had noticed the letter in the hand of the statue. He had also noticed that it was not there when he had visited the church earlier that morning. A thought occurred to him.

"Perhaps we should have a closer look at the letter," he said.

Dona Dante did not immediately take his meaning, but she followed the sacristan to the front of the church, where he suggested she take the letter from St. Anthony's hand. When she did, gold coins began to tumble out of a coin purse tucked inside the statue's sleeve. Three hundred *escudos* in all! A fortune!

Senora Dante opened the letter and felt faint. Before she read a word, she recognized her husband's handwriting. There could be no doubt: the letter was from her beloved Antonio.

The sacristan helped her to take a seat in the first pew. There she quietly read her husband's letter.

Lima, July 23, 1729

My Dear Wife,

For some time, I have been expecting a letter from you. I have been greatly troubled at not hearing from you. At last, one of the Franciscan fathers has delivered your letter, and given me great joy! I am sending this response by the same religious. I enclosed three hundred *escudos* for your support until I return . . .

St. Anthony's Chapel has a tooth from St. Anthony of Padua on display in case ZC along the left side of the chapel as you face the altar. There are far too many stories about St. Anthony to tell them all here. I have selected these particular stories to introduce readers to St. Anthony, to introduce some of the lesser known stories about him, and to explain the origin of some of the traditions and practices associated with him. The tradition of asking St. Anthony to help find lost things seems to have originated with the theft of his psalter and his prayer for its return. We know from his contemporary Julian of Spires that people began praying for Anthony to help them find lost things shortly after his death. The tradition of writing S.A.G., or "St. Anthony Guide," on letters has its origin in the story of Dona and Antonio Dante. St. Anthony was known, even during his lifetime, as a wonder-worker and as the Hammer of Heretics. He had a great devotion to the Blessed Mother. He died in 1231, at the age of thirty five. His feast day is June 13th. St. Anthony of Padua has many patronages, and his intercession is often sought to help find lost items and missing people, as well as to protect against shipwreck.

St. Mark the Evangelist

The ship slid into its mooring, and a wooden walkway was lowered into position. The passengers were allowed to disembark first. Afterward, the crew would unload the cargo and then begin their shore leave.

Mark walked down the gangway. He had arrived in the western harbor. In the distance, on the other side of the Heptastadion, he could see the famous lighthouse. Mark stepped onto the wharf. As he did so, his sandal strap broke. "Ah," he thought. "I am just arrived in Alexandria, and my first order of business is to find a cobbler! I hope this is not a sign of things to come."

Mark had been reluctant to come to Egypt. Had the request not come from Peter himself, he would have found an excuse to remain in Italy, despite the recent tensions and emperor Claudius' order expelling the Jews from the city of Rome. He thought to himself, "Aquileia is still safe. Perhaps I should have gone there," but he put this thought out of mind as soon as it came to him. Peter wanted him here, so he needed to be here.

There were, of course, small Christian communities in other parts of Egypt, but Alexandria was truly new territory for the Church. Mark had no illusions about this assignment. His work here, in this great center of pagan learning and worldliness, would not be easy.

The waterfront was crowded and noisy.

The day was hot. It was afternoon, and the sun was still high overhead, shining brightly in a cloudless sky. Sunlight reflected brightly off of the endless white stucco buildings that made up the city: government offices, pagan temples, theaters, even shops and houses, all shared the same rounded corners and soft white exteriors.

In a narrow alley just off the quay, Mark found a leatherworker and approached him regarding his sandal. The man was very friendly. He introduced himself as Anianus, and he assured Mark that yes, of course he could cut and fit a new strap for Mark's sandal.

Anianus was much younger than Mark. He had only recently completed his apprenticeship and entered fully into his trade. His hair was dark. His beard was neatly trimmed, and he had a broad, engaging smile.

Anianus worked from a little collapsible stall attached to the front of his house, and he invited Mark to wait inside while he worked.

"Come, friend," he said, as he pulled back a heavy wool curtain and motioned Mark in through an open doorway. "It will be maybe a quarter of an hour before your sandal is ready. You are welcome to wait here."

Anianus' wife was inside, but she quickly disappeared as soon as Mark entered, and he found himself alone in a small but comfortable room. The room was windowless and a little dark, but much cooler than outside.

Mark sat down on a wooden bench next to a low table set with fresh flowers. Mark could smell food cooking somewhere nearby, and he realized that he was hungry. From somewhere in the back of the house, or perhaps in the courtyard behind it, Mark could hear children laughing and calling to one another as they played.

A moment later, Anianus' wife returned. She had anticipated his needs. Mark looked up as she silently placed some fresh *labneh* and a small plate with a few dates and olives on the table in front of him. He smiled and nodded his thanks.

Anianus tied back the curtain so that see could see Mark as he worked. He took out a square of leather and set it on his cutting table. Then he placed a drop of oil on the rounded blade of his saddler knife, and began to work the knife back and forth along his strop. As he worked he spoke to Mark.

"You are new to the city?" he asked.

"Yes," Mark replied.

"Where are you from, my friend?" he continued.

"I have travelled throughout the empire, but I am newly arrived here from Rome," Mark replied.

"Ah! One God!" the man cried suddenly. His knife had slipped, and he had cut himself deeply! The injury was serious. Mark acted quickly. He raced through the house to the rear courtyard, where he found a small garden. From the garden, he scooped up a handful of loose soil. Then he spat into his hand two or three times to make a paste.

He could hear the Anianus' wife screaming, Her screams were followed by shouts from neighbors and the sound of feet running down the narrow alleyway as the alarm was raised.

Mark returned as quickly as he could to the injured leatherworker. A crowd had started to assemble around the little stall. Mark applied his paste to man's cut. Immediately the blood flow slowed. Within a few minutes it had stopped, and soon the wound was visibly starting to heal. Anianus looked on, as astonished as the people around him. His breathing slowly returned to normal, and his wife calmed down as she realized that the danger had passed.

Just then, a neighbor arrived with a doctor who was not pleased to find that his services were no longer needed. He left in a huff. Then Anianus turned to Mark.

"Friend, I do not know how to thank you!" He said with genuine gratitude. Then his expression changed, and he looked puzzled. "How very strange, isn't it?" he said quietly and to no one in particular.

"What is strange?" asked Mark. "That you should be healed?"

"That, yes!" replied the young tradesman, "But when I cut my hand, I cried out, 'One God!'" replied the leatherworker. "What a strange thing for me to say! 'One God,' why should I say that? What could it even mean?" asked Anianus.

Mark understood. "I believe I can answer that," he said with a smile. "It was a sign, a communication of the Spirit, to let me know that my broken sandal has led me to the right place."

"I do not understand," replied the Anianus.

"I am a servant of Christ Jesus," said Mark.

"I do not know him. Is he here in the city?" asked Anianus.

"Come inside, friend, we have much to discuss," replied Mark. Then they went into the house, and Anianus's wife finished preparing the evening meal. When the food was ready, Anianus and his family sat down at table with Mark, and he began to teach them about Jesus.

*   *   *

Buono and Rustico were merchants, but they had not come to Alexandria to trade. They had come to commit a crime. These two men of Venice, who normally trafficked in oil and spice, were now in Egypt to take delivery of a very different, and very special, cargo.

Buono was the older of the two. He was heavyset, with a full beard. Rustico was younger. He was thin, with long, dark hair heavily treated with oil.

Both men wore wide-sleeved embroidered silk coats over tunics made from expensive Indian cotton. Their coats were heavily decorated in blue and green floral patterns, with great, long tails that reached down behind their knees. Buono wore a matching felt cap. Both men wore wide leather belts, tight fitting woolen trousers, and long-toed leather slippers adorned with gold leaf.

Their clothing was inappropriate for the climate of Egypt, and it marked them as wealthy foreigners. For their ruse to work, however, it would be important for the Caliph's men to recognize them as Venetian merchants at the appropriate time.

It was early morning. Buono guessed that they had maybe half an hour until sunrise. The two men needed to move quickly, and they needed to be careful. There were few people out at this early hour, and the two men understood that any of them might be tempted to assault two wealthy merchants foolish enough to wander down the wrong alley.

Buono and Rustico walked in silence through an endless maze of narrow streets crowded with produce carts, tent stalls, reed baskets, water jars, hanging laundry, and piles of household trash. Flies swarmed and rats scurried. There were chamber pots outside of every door. Some had been emptied, others still awaited collection by the night soil man.

Buono frequently reached into one of his oversized pockets for a bone to quiet the dogs that, now and again, threatened to call too much attention to their passing.

Rustico kept his hand on his dagger.

As they walked, the two traders made a few intentional wrong turns to disguise their movements and lose anyone who might be following. They were, of course, on their way to a suspicious destination. They were on their way to a church.

* * *

Mark was getting ready to say Mass. He groaned under his breath. He was getting on in years. To be sure, he still had remarkable energy and zeal for the Gospel, but he was now burdened with innumerable little aches and pains. Mark paused to reflect, and he realized that he had been preaching the Gospel in Alexandria for nearly twenty years now. The Christian community he had founded all those years ago had grown dramatically, and he smiled to himself as he remembered its humble beginnings in the home of Anianus the cobbler.

The Christians of Alexandria now worshiped in a beautiful church overlooking the eastern harbor.

The growing number of Christians alarmed the pagan authorities. Their priests hated Mark for his preaching against their idols, and they began to plot against him. Word of their plans reached Mark, and he understood that soon he would follow in the footsteps of Stephen, Peter, Paul, and so many others.

There was a knock at the door.

"Come in," Mark said.

The door opened, and Anianus entered with a smile. Mark studied his old friend. Anianus had put on weight. His hair had thinned, but it was still dark, and his smile was unchanged.

"How are the grandchildren?" Mark asked.

"All well. All well. You wanted to see me?" replied Anianus.

"Yes," Mark said quietly. "The priests of Serapis plot against us, and Nero still reigns in Rome."

Anianus nodded. "Yes, these are dark times for Christ's church," he answered.

Mark paused for a moment, and then spoke, "The Egyptians, the Romans, the Jews, old age . . . one way or another, my time grows short. We need to plan for the future of the church here in Alexandria. I have always believed the Holy Spirit arranged for me to meet you when I arrived. Your family were the first in Alexandria to be baptized, and you have remained by my side ever since. It is only natural that you should succeed me as Bishop of Alexandria."

*   *   *

The Christian population of Egypt had faced persecution since the Moslem conquest two hundred years earlier, but the situation had recently become acute. The Caliph had embarked on an ambitious building program. He was looting and dismantling Christian churches for materials to use in the construction of his palaces and mosques. The Christian heritage of the city was slowly being wiped away. The Christian art and artifacts that remained were now in great danger. They could be confiscated, or simply destroyed, at any time.

Buono and Rustico arrived at the church. The church was large and square. It was made of white stucco over sundried mudbrick, with a high roofline, and several copper copulas, each sporting a Coptic cross. The church was beautiful in the waning moonlight, and the two men of Venice took just a second to admire it before proceeding down a narrow walkway to a side entrance.

Two elderly priests dressed in long black robes and tight-fitting *koulla* hoods met Buono and Rustico and opened the door. They quickly ushered the two merchants through a high arch and into a long hall. The priests had previously arranged for the delivery of a large, rigid wicker hamper with a hinged lid and rope handles. Two Christian porters stood nearby awaiting instructions. Buono looked quickly inside the hamper to confirm that it had been loaded. He nodded, and the two porters took up their positions on either end of the straw-plaited crate.

The two porters exited the church with Buono and Rustico in tow. The four men walked around to the front of the church, where they entered onto a broad avenue that sloped gently down to the wharf. They walked slowly and deliberately toward the docks. As they went, the two porters called out, "Pork, unclean! Pork, unclean!" and the few runners and warehousemen, who had made an early start to their day gave them a wide berth.

The church was not far from the waterfront. The porters covered the distance in less than ten minutes. Soon Buono and Rustico could see the shadowy outlines of countless ships sheltering inside the protective breakwater that stretched from the quayside to the lighthouse. Buono directed the porter's attention down the docks to a particular ship moored for lading. The men on board were moving a gangplank into position. The ship would soon be ready to take on freight.

The porters began to carry the hamper toward the waiting ship. Then, as expected, two customs officials stepped forward to stop them. The porters sat the hamper down. The inspectors directed the porters to open it. The porters then threw open the lid to reveal salted pork and cabbage, and the two duty agents recoiled in horror at the sight of the butchered pigs.

"*Haram, Haram!*" cried the younger of the two officials.

Just then, the sun appeared on the horizon. An instant later, the morning call to prayer went out from every minaret in the city. With a wave, the more senior official directed the porters to load their profane consignment. Then the two duty agents hurried off to the mosque, never so happy to attend to their prayers.

Buono suppressed a smile. Their subterfuge had worked. The Caliph's men had not questioned the arrival of two well-dressed foreign merchants carrying forbidden foodstuffs, and their timing had been perfect. They had been allowed to board their ship without having to unload the hamper or answer any troublesome questions.

Buono silently offered a brief prayer of thanks.

Buono and Rustico paid the two porters, who then departed. The Venetian crew worked very efficiently. The mooring lines were untied, the walkway was withdrawn, and the rowers began to maneuver the ship out of the harbor. When the ship was free of the breakwater, the oars were stowed, the sails were raised, and soon the coastline of Egypt was receding into the distance.

St. Mark the Evangelist

*   *   *

Mark was waiting the when the mob came for him. There were hundreds of them: young and old, men and women, all shouting curses against Mark and his God. Mark recognized a few priests of Serapis among them. They were distinguished by their shaved heads, powdered faces, and kohl-black eyes. The priests were moving among the people, inciting them to anger.

At the urging of the priests, the angry crowd fell upon Mark, and in an instant he felt a rope tighten around his neck. He was pulled from his feet. He grabbed at the noose and struggled to breathe as the crowd began to drag him through the city. He turned this way and that as he was dragged over the crushed stone paving. Soon he was a mass of blood and broken bone. His eyes swelled shut, and his neck burned with each tug of the rope.

The crowd laughed and roared its approval. "Take him to the butcher," they cried, as the men among them dragged Mark through the city.

In time, the crowd tired of their sport, and Mark was thrown into prison. The prison was dark, and it smelled of illness and death. Mark found himself alone and in great pain, but he did not despair. He simply prayed. Then, in early morning hours, he became of aware of a light in his cell. An angel had come to comfort him.

The angel spoke. "Peace be upon you, Mark. Don't be afraid. You have shown great courage so far. Know that I will be with you the rest of the way."

As the angel spoke, Mark felt the pain leave his body, though his injuries remained.

St. Mark the Evangelist

In the morning, the jailer took Mark from his cell and handed him back over to the crowd. Once more, the priests of Serapis called upon the crowd to drag the Christian to his death. Once more, Mark felt the burn of the rope around his neck. Once more, the crowd dragged him through the city, but this time he felt no pain. Mark was already halfway to heaven. When his final moment arrived, he repeated the words of his Lord and Master, "Into your hands, I commend my spirit." With that he died.

The sun disappeared, and the sky turned dark! There was a crack of thunder and a gust of wind as a beautiful morning suddenly and unexpectedly gave way to a violent storm. A hard rain mixed with hail poured down from the heavens and quickly dispersed the crowd. The priests of Serapis had planned to burn Mark's body, for they knew it was Christian practice to bury their dead and they wished to deny Mark this privilege. For a second or two, the priests lingered behind the others, their makeup running down their wet faces. Then they too ran for the shelter of their temple, like rats to their holes, and Mark's body was left lying in the street.

Anianus had instructed the Christians not to interfere with Mark's martyrdom, but several of them had followed discretely behind the crowd. When the pagan mob melted away into the rain, they saw their chance. Three men sprang from the shadows. They rushed to Mark's aid, and when they confirmed that he was dead, they carried him back to the church, and informed Anianus that he was now bishop.

*   *   *

St. Mark the Evangelist

Buono and Rustico took off their coats and tunics. Stripped to the waist, they opened the hamper and began to scoop out armfuls of pork and cabbage preserved in salt and seasoned with herbs.

"Ah, the smell!" cried Rustico. "Maybe the Moors are right. Maybe we should not touch the pig!"

"Quit worrying about the smell. Just clear out the hamper," Buono said sternly.

A minute later, they reached the bottom of the hamper. There they found the mummy still wrapped in linen. They carefully removed the mummy and laid it on the deck. Then they unwrapped soiled linens to reveal the desiccated human remains within.

"So, it is true?" asked Rustico. "I confess, I only half believed."

"Yes, it is true," replied Buono.

The two men studied the precious relic. The remains were male, and still bore obvious evidence of the injuries the man had sustained on that day long ago, when a mob had seized him, placed a rope around his neck, and dragged him to his death through the streets of Alexandria.

They lovingly and carefully washed his dry and brittle corpse. Then they carefully re-wrapped it in a bit of sail and stowed it for passage.

Buono took a moment to pray, *"Marcus, ora pro nobis,"* before returning to his duties aboard ship. The captain gave his orders. The halyards were tensioned, the jib was trimmed, the mainsail was set to close haul, and the Venetian vessel tacked sharply westward, as it began its return journey to Venice . . . And that is how the relics of St. Mark the Evangelist came to the floating city.

St. Mark the Evangelist

St. Anthony's Chapel has bone fragments from St. Mark the Evangelist on display in cases ZA, ZB, and V. St. Mark the Evangelist is best known as the author of the second Gospel. However, he also helped to found the church at Alexandria in Egypt, and he served there as bishop for many years. He was martyred in 68 A.D. The Book of Revelation describes four living creatures who surround the throne of God (Rev 4:7). Early church tradition associates these creatures with the four evangelists. This why the winged lion has become a symbol of St. Mark. His feast day is April 25th. He is the patron saint of Egypt and of the City of Venice.

S. MARK, EVANGELIST.
From the Vienna Missal.

St. Fina dei Caeri

It was late morning when little Bella heard men shouting outside. She pushed open a wooden shutter and looked down onto the street below.

"*Mammina*, who are those men?" she asked.

Her mother came over to look. Then she gasped and pulled her young daughter away from the window. She covered Bella's eyes with one hand and quickly closed the shutter with the other. "Don't look. Don't look," she whispered. She tried to sound reassuring, but Bella heard the strain in her mother's voice.

Louisa's husband Paolo entered the room. "What is it, Louisa?" he asked.

"They're here, Paolo," she said.

Paolo opened the shutter an inch and peaked outside. When he closed the shutter, his expression was grim, and the blood drained from his face.

"We must go to her," he said.

*　　*　　*

The men were stripped to the waist, and covered in ash. They beat themselves with whips and bound themselves with cords and chains. They wandered through the city banging on doors and windows, wild-eyed penitents who had come to proclaim God's imminent judgment.

"The Day of Judgment is at hand! Even now, wickedness corrupts your flesh!" they cried.

Everyone in San Gimignano had heard the stories. Now they knew the stories were true. The plague had returned.

*   *   *

The residents of San Gimignano responded differently to the news that the plague had returned. Some thought to flee. Others shut themselves up in their shops and houses, desperately hoping this outbreak would pass them by. Still others sought to occupy their final days before damnation with drunkenness and pleasures of the flesh.

A few, however, decided to pray.

Bella and her parents made their way to the Piazza della Cisterna, where a handful of people had already assembled. The day was cloudy, and the tower houses, which normally defined the skyline, merged almost seamlessly into the leaden sky.

Near the center of the plaza, old Father Bartolo was giving orders, trying to organize this anxious gathering into an orderly procession as the wind blew his wispy white hair into a tangled mess.

Eventually everyone quieted down and fell into line behind their elderly priest. Then Father Bartolo began to lead them through the narrow cobblestone streets of the town center to a tiny chapel, the final resting place of a young girl who had suffered unimaginably and who had faithfully offered up her suffering for the people of this picturesque town known for its turrets and spires. Along their route, lingering puddles testified to the rain that had fallen overnight, and downed branches littered the streets.

With as much reassurance as he could muster, old Father Bartolo called to the men and women behind him, "Come, come. Stay close. Follow me. Follow me."

*   *   *

The plague men did not stay long. By afternoon, they were on their way to the next little Tuscan town, and the streets of San Gimignano fell silent, save for the scurrying of the rats, the little harbingers of death appointed by God as agents of his divine fury.

*   *   *

Inside the chapel, Bella, her parents, and the other faithful gathered close around the altar as two young boys lit candles and oil lamps. Father Bartolo said a short prayer. Then he told them the following story:

"Brothers and sisters, as we pray for God's mercy, let us remember our patron saint. St. Fina was born here in San Gimignano. She was a pretty little girl, who had a happy childhood, until she fell ill at age ten. She contracted a slow spreading paralysis, from which she never recovered.

"St. Fina lost her father at age twelve, and her mother at fourteen.

"St. Fina was confined to a simple board on the floor of her room, able only to move her head and neck. Her one possession was a crucifix on the wall.

"She spent her days in prayer. In the evening, a neighbor and a childhood friend would visit. They brought her what little food she received and did what they could to care for her. They spent an hour or so with her each day. The rest of the time, she was alone.

"Fina was a person of extraordinary faith, who remembered the words of St. Paul, 'For now I rejoice in my sufferings, for by them I complete what is lacking in Christ's suffering, for the sake of his body, that is, the church.'"You see, Fina understood that she had been called to serve Christ through her suffering, and this she did. She devoted her life to prayer, fasting, and the patient endurance of her condition, as a service for the people of this, her beloved hometown. She kept her faith. She kept her resolve, even in the late hours of the night, when the rats came and gnawed on her fingers and toes.

"St. Fina shared her days with the angels and saints. She had a great devotion to Pope St. Gregory the Great, who appeared to her shortly before her death. He told her to be ready, for on his feast day, she would rise to heaven.

"A few days later, she died as predicted. When her body was carried from her room, the church bells rang, and the entire city erupted in a profusion of white violets, all suddenly in bloom. The appearance of so many flowers in bloom, so early in the season, was counted a miracle and taken as confirmation that young Fina had indeed entered into glory."

*   *   *

As Father Bartolo told the faithful the story of St. Fina and asked them to pray for her intercession, a miracle occurred, though no one noticed at the time. It would be some weeks before anyone realized what had happened, or more precisely, what had not happened. As the people in the chapel asked St. Fina to pray for them and for the town she loved, the pale horseman passed on by, continuing on his way to the next town. The rest of Tuscany burned with fever, but no plague came to San Gimignano.

Most of St. Fina's relics reside in the St. Fina Chapel in San Gimignano, Italy, but St. Anthony's Chapel does have a relic from her in case U, just to the left of the altar. St. Fina died in 1253. She was 15 years old. Her feast day is March 12th. She shares her feast day with Pope St. Gregory the Great, to whom she had a special devotion. She is remembered for her patient suffering. In Catholic thought, we are meant to experience some suffering, which we are asked to join to Christ's suffering on the cross. This idea of redemptive suffering is important to understanding why Fina dei Caeri is regarded as a saint. She is the patron saint of her hometown of San Gimignano, Italy, which is still known today for its surviving Medieval architecture, including many of its famous tower houses.

St. Isidore the Farmer

L ong ago, in the days when Alfonso was Emperor of Spain, there lived a man named Isidore, who worked as a farmhand amid the rolling hills and rocky mesas of southern Castile. There, in the Valley of the Manzanares, Isidore made his home within view of the distant Guadaramma Mountains and the old Moorish citadel of Al-Mudayah that still kept watch over the countryside.

Isidore was a giant of a man, and driving the oxen through his master's fields had once left him strong and fit. The passage of time, however, had started to take its inevitable toll. He could no longer furrow a field in a day and his labors left him sore and aching. He could feel the advancing years in his bones and see them in the greying of his beard.

Not far from Isidore's cottage, there was a small stone church. The church was old and falling into ruin. The bell tower was empty, so there was no call to prayer and no peal to mark the beginning and end of the workday. Still, the church opened early each morning so that those who wished could attend Mass or say a few prayers. Many ploughmen and corkers began their day in this way, and it was Isidore's custom to rise early and walk to the little church regardless of weather or season.

Isidore was a man of exceptional piety, a piety that earned him the enmity of some of his co-workers. They made jokes at his expense and complained to the landowner that Isidore spent too much time in prayer and not enough time behind the plow.

Still, Isidore was well-liked by most of the people who knew him. He was also known for his charity and was never reluctant to share what little he had with a friend, or a neighbor, or a stranger in need.

Though he rarely thought of himself, Isidore had one deeply held personal wish. He wished to make a pilgrimage to the Holy Land. He wished to see all the places named in the gospels: Bethlehem and Nazareth and Capernaum and Jerusalem - the places where Our Lord lived and preached and endured His passion. Poverty and age, however, meant that it was now very unlikely that Isidore would ever have an opportunity to travel so far from home.

Late one summer day, when the fields were a golden sea of ripening grain and the strawberry trees[2] were in bloom, Isidore made his way home to find a beggar waiting at his door. The man was old and spindly with bare feet and long, wispy white hair that wafted about his head with each passing breeze. His broad and crooked smile revealed a handful of broken yellow teeth, all crooked and ready to give way. Over a rough and tattered tunic, he wore a thin burlap cloak wrapped tightly about his person in the fashion of a pilgrim. In his right hand he carried a long staff, and over his shoulder he wore a scrip on a long leather strap. On a course string tied about his waist he wore a pierced scallop shell that identified him as a man on his way to Santiago de Compostella.

The stranger did not identify himself, but begged a little food

---

2   Strawberry trees are species of tree native to the Iberian Peninsula. They produce a fruit that looks a lot like a strawberry. A strawberry tree is featured on the flag for the city of Madrid.

and shelter for the night. Isidore invited him in, lit a fire, and prepared a meager supper for the two of them to share. He could only offer a little cheese, a little wine, and some thin barley gruel, but the pilgrim accepted these gratefully, and the two men sat down to eat.

As they ate, Isidore asked the pilgrim about his travels. The pilgrim was indeed on his way to Santiago de Compostella, but he had spent most of the last three years in the Holy Land, where he had visited all of the places that Isidore most longed to see. The stranger told Isidore of the ancient and mysterious pyramids of Egypt, of the desert wilderness of the Sinai, and of the strange salinity of the Dead Sea. However, it was his description of the sites associated with the ministry of Jesus that most intrigued Isidore. Again and again, Isidore asked the elderly pilgrim to tell him about Bethany beyond the Jordan where John lived, and Cana where Jesus attended the wedding feast, and Jacob's well where Our Lord spoke with the Samaritan woman. Again and again the old man patiently answered Isidore's questions in great detail. He described the perfumed scent of the red and gold wildflowers blooming across the hillside where Jesus had preached the Sermon on the Mount, and the dark silhouette of Mt. Tabor rising abruptly against the afternoon sky in the Jezreel Valley. He spoke of the little fish that swim in the warm, clear spring at Caesarea Phillipi where Peter first identified Jesus as the Christ, and on and on until he had vividly recounted every detail of all of the places that he had visited.

The two men talked well into the night, but in time they grew tired. The fire began to fade, and Isidore drifted off to sleep. It wasn't long, however, before he found himself awake and standing on a hillside. He was startled by a voice from behind him.

"This way, my friend," said the voice.

When Isidore turned around, he saw a young man dressed in fine robes, who glowed with a celestial light. The young man seemed oddly familiar. Then suddenly, Isidore realized that the young man was the old pilgrim, now transformed, magnificent, and radiant like the sun - clearly an angel sent by the Lord!

The angel spoke to Isidore.

"This is the field where shepherds first heard that the Savior had been born," said the angel. Then the angel pointed off in the distance.

Isidore looked to see a dusty little village: a humble place of rough stone houses and dusty streets, where the sound of baying animals and a constant clang of sheep bells filled the air, a village that could only be Bethlehem. An instant later, Isidore found himself much nearer to the village. He was standing in front of a little cave that served as a stable. There were no animals at present, but the floor of the cave was littered with straw.

The angel smiled and said simply, "The manger," and Isidore understood that this was the place where the Savior had been born.

The angel waved his hand and the two of them were at once transported to Nazareth. After that, they flew to Capernaum, where they walked along the shore of the Sea of Galilee, and then instantly on to Jerusalem. There they saw the site of the old temple, and the Mount of Olives, and came as near as they could to the former site of the Antonia Fortress, and the Praetorium where Jesus was scourged and sentenced to death.

As they made their way down the Via Dolorosa, following the Way of Sorrow, the angel recited the Stations of the Cross until they came to Golgotha where Jesus had suffered on the cross.

Finally, the angel concluded the tour with a stop at the ruined Church of the Holy Sepulcher, which had only recently been reopened to pilgrims. There Isidore saw the tomb where Jesus had been laid to rest and where he rose again on the third day.

When Isidore had seen everything that his heart desired, the angel reached out and touched him on the forehead.

"Remember and believe!" the angel commanded.

Then Isidore awoke. He looked around and found himself alone in his little cottage. The old pilgrim was gone, the fire had died out, and the first rays of the rising sun were just now starting to shine through the windows.

Everything was as it should have been at the start of a new workday, everything except Isidore. For Isidore understood perfectly well that his experience had been no mere dream, that he had indeed been allowed, by a special grace, to make his pilgrimage, and he was profoundly grateful. With tears in his eyes, he resolved to make this morning's Mass a time of special thanksgiving. He rose, took a few minutes to ready himself, and then set off for the half-ruined little stone chapel.

St. Anthony's Chapel has relics from St. Isidore the Farmer on display in cases G and Z along the right side of the chapel as you face the altar. St. Isidore is remembered for his simple piety. He reminds us that we are all called to be saints. When his body was accidentally exhumed by a flood forty years after his death, it was found to be incorrupt. There are many charming legends regarding St. Isidore, including the story of his miraculous pilgrimage. WAOB Audio Theatre has recorded a slightly different version of this story under the title "The Grateful Pilgrim."

St. Isidore the Farmer

St. Isidore the Farmer has many patronages including farmers, laborers, and the city of Madrid, Spain. He died in 1130. His feast day is May 15th.

St. Benedict the Abbot

St. Benedict loved his brothers, but he also missed his life as a hermit, so now and again he would leave the monastery and head off into the surrounding woods to spend a few days alone, living as he had lived during his time as a young man in Subiaco.

One fall morning, as Benedict was preparing for one of his trips into the woods, a loaf of bread arrived at the monastery. The bread was a gift to Benedict from a priest named Florentius. Benedict required his monastery to be self-sufficient, but it was still common for people to give alms to the brothers, and small gifts, such as a loaf of bread, were gratefully accepted.

Benedict liked to share little bits of his bread with a raven. The raven was quite beautiful, with a sheen to its black feathers that would reflect a hint of blue when the light was just right. The raven came to visit Benedict each day. In time, it became quite tame, and Benedict came to see the bird as a kind of pet. The two formed a close bond, and Benedict was empowered, by a special grace, to make himself understood by his friend the raven.

Benedict thought to share the bread he had received from Florentius with the raven, but something was not right. When Benedict made the sign of the cross over the bread, as was his custom, the Holy Spirit revealed to him that the bread had been poisoned!

A short time later, the raven arrived emerged from the woods, looking to share Benedict's morning meal.

Benedict spoke to the raven. "Take this bread, and dispose of it where it will it not harm anyone!"

At first, the raven refused to carry the poisoned loaf away. It cawed, shrieked, and leapt about in protest. Benedict spoke softly to the bird until it calmed down. Eventually, it took the bread in it beak and flew off to parts unknown.

Benedict resumed his preparations for some time alone in the woods. He gathered some grain and vegetables and put them into a coarse burlap sack. Then he set off for his favorite spot. The woods were beautiful and full of life. The goodness of creation always left Benedict with a renewed sense of purpose and restored his enthusiasm for his work.

Three hours later, Benedict arrived in a beautiful little valley ringed by low hills. The hills were covered with trees of various kinds, stands of tall grass, and wild sunflowers. The sun was shining, and Benedict found a shady spot to rest under a large fig tree heavy with ripe fruit.

Benedict scratched his mostly bald head, smiled, and whistled softly as he helped himself to a few figs.

A short while later, the raven found Benedict, and he shared some of his grain with the hungry bird.

As Benedict sat under the fig tree, he thought about Florentius and the poisoned bread. Benedict knew that some of the brothers found his rules too strict. They plotted against him. One or two hoped to succeed him as abbot. Benedict understood that Florentius must have similar designs.

Benedict really wanted some time alone but, upon reflection, he decided that he should return to the monastery. He did not know whether Florentius had acted alone. He preferred to keep the matter of the poisoned bread quiet, but he realized that he would need to personally reassure the majority of brothers who supported him, should it become known that an attempt had been made on his life.

It was late afternoon when Benedict arrived back at the monastery. As Benedict approached the gate, it suddenly flew open, and one of the brothers came running out to meet him. It was Brother Constantinus, and he was very excited.

"Abba Benedict! Dear brother! Is it really you? Are you well?" Constantinus asked with great concern.

"Yes, Constantinus. I am fine," replied Benedict.

"Oh, thank God! Oh, thank God!" continued Constantinus. "It's the priest Florentius! He plots against you! He poisoned your bread! He planned for you to die alone in the woods. It is his ambition to succeed you as abbot . . . we had no way to reach you . . . all we could do was pray! We were sure you were dead! Ah, but God has heard our prayers!"

Benedict interrupted. "Dear Constantius, there was never any danger. The Holy Spirit revealed to me that the bread was poisoned, and with the help of my friend the raven, I was spared. As for Florentius, we do not need worry about him. God has revealed to me that He will soon address this transgression."

St. Anthony's Chapel has several relics from St. Benedict the Abbot on display in various cases around the chapel. St. Benedict is considered the father of Western monasticism. He wrote The Rule of St. Benedict, *which governs life in most religious communities to this day. There are many colorful stories about St. Benedict. The earliest version of the story of the raven seems to have been written by St. Gregory the Great in his*

St. Benedict the Abbot

Dialogues around 593. It speaks to Benedict's holiness and receipt of special graces. According to St. Gregory, the priest Florentius died soon after his attempt to poison St. Benedict, when the building he was in partially collapsed. St. Benedict remains a very popular saint. He is often depicted in art with a raven. The famous St. Benedict medal was first struck in 1880, but the symbols on the medal are much older. St. Benedict died in 543. He has many patronages and is invoked against poisoning. His feast day is March 21st.

S. BENEDICT. After Cahier.

[March 21.

St. Lawrence of Rome

Emperor Decius paced back and forth, his face red with anger. Only a week ago, Decius had won a great victory when he defeated Emperor Philip and the few legions still loyal to him. The two rivals had clashed near Verona. After his decisive victory, Decius marched his troops south. Earlier today, they had arrived in Rome and publicly proclaimed Decius emperor.

Decius was nearing fifty. He wore his hair closely cropped and kept his upper lip and chin clean-shaven. After years fighting the Goths, he preferred boots to sandals, and he was fond of heavy wool tunics, which he usually kept closed with a large, gold brooch fastened tight against his right shoulder.

It was after midnight when Decius sent soldiers out to rouse as many quaestors, senators, and prefects as possible from their beds. The officials now assembled before him now were still half asleep.

The emperor pointed to a large empty vault behind him and shouted, "I have made a most disturbing discovery! Emperor Philip filled this vault with treasure! Now it is empty! Where is the treasure? Where is the tribute?"

For a moment, no one said a word.

Then Decius continued, "I'll tell you where it is! Philip handed it over to the Christians for safekeeping before riding out to meet me on the battlefield! I always suspected . . . prepare a decree! All Romans must make a public sacrifice to our ancestral gods, and will receive a certificate upon completion of the sacrifice. This will flush out the Christians! I want their property confiscated and their priests executed until we recover the treasure they are hiding! It is the property of the Roman state!"

*   *   *

Pope Sixtus and all seven deacons of Rome had been quickly arrested and executed. Only the seventh deacon remained. His name was Lawrence.

Lawrence was a Spaniard. He was tall and handsome. Still in his twenties, his hair and beard were full and black. Lawrence was trim, with deep-set intelligent brown eyes, and he was known for his wry sense of humor.

Lawrence was also the deacon responsible for the keeping of Church funds and for overseeing the distribution of alms to the poor.

Emperor Decius wanted to interview him personally.

Prefect Hippolytus was given custody of Lawrence. Prefect Hippolytus held Lawrence in the basement of an old house that now served as a makeshift prison. The prison was very dark. The air was close and stale. At times it was hard to breath. Here Lawrence counted down the days, waiting to be summoned to appear before the emperor.

Lawrence shared the basement with another prisoner, a blind old pagan named Lucillius. Lucillius was very thin and wore only a filthy, threadbare cloth about his waist. His nails were broken, his teeth were missing, and his long hair hung down in front of his face.

Lucillius had no family. He was uneducated, and his life had been very hard, but he was also an inherently good man who refused to give in to anger, bitterness, or despair.

Lucillius found himself very drawn to Lawrence, and he questioned the deacon extensively about Christianity until one day, blind old Lucillius made a profession of faith and asked to be baptized. Whereupon Deacon Lawrence received him into the Church with a handful of water from a basin.

Prefect Hippolytus witnessed the baptism of Lucillius and was deeply moved.

*   *   *

When Lawrence was finally brought before the tribunal, he promised to surrender all of the treasure the Church possessed if the emperor would give him three days to gather the treasure together.

Prefect Hippolytus vouched for Lawrence, and Emperor Decius granted this request.

*   *   *

Prefect Hippolytus looked out over the balcony. The morning sun was still low in the sky, and Hippolytus found himself squinting against the glare from the reflecting pool in the courtyard below. It would be uncomfortably warm by afternoon but, for the moment, the air was still cool and pleasant. Somewhere in the distance, Hippolytus could hear the laughter and excited cries of children at play in the garden.

The prefect turned and walked back into the chamber where the tribunal would meet. The walls of the chamber were densely decorated with murals depicting scenes from Roman mythology. Hippolytus found himself staring absentmindedly at an image of the she-wolf nursing Romulus and Remus. The image was outlined in heavy black and colored in contrasting whites, browns, and burgundies.

Several lanterns hung suspended from the ceiling. A statue of Minerva looked on in silence as oily smoke curled up from one of the lanterns to slowly form a dark, sooty spot above the cathedra.

As Hippolytus stood lost in thought, slaves and functionaries came and went, attending to the food, wine, and incense that would be needed for the meeting of the tribunal and the colloquy that would follow.

Hippolytus wore the purple border of officialdom around the edge of the white toga that he draped loosely over his tunic. At forty, he was still fit, and only the greying around his temples hinted at his encroaching middle age. In this insular world, everything seemed perfect, though at present Hippolytus took no pleasure in his wealth or privileged station.

The deacon would be here soon, and Hippolytus was not looking forward to their reunion. Three days had passed and Hippolytus had now returned to the Sallustian Palace for the resumption of the interrogation. He did not doubt that Deacon Lawrence would surrender himself as promised, but he could not deny that there was a part of him that hoped the deacon would flee. Hippolytus had developed a fondness for Lawrence and for his strange teachings.

St. Lawrence of Rome

*　　*　　*

Emperor Decius and the other members of the tribunal made their way into the hall and took their seats upon the dais. A few minutes later, there was a knock upon the door. A guard opened the door, and Lawrence walked into the chamber. He stood before the tribunal, but he was not alone. Lawrence was accompanied by a motley assortment of dirty beggars, lepers, orphans, elderly, and people with disabilities, who had come to stand with him before the emperor.

When Decius asked Lawrence to explain the meaning of this assembly, Lawrence replied, "I bring you the treasure of the Church! These people are our treasure, a treasure which never diminishes, but grows and grows, shared by all and carried by each to Heaven."

Emperor Decius was furious. He turned to the guards and said, "Torture him until evening, then bring him back to me!"

For his insult to the tribunal, Lawrence was first scourged, then beaten with clubs, then stung by scorpions, and finally burned with swords heated in a fire.

*　　*　　*

That evening, Lawrence was again brought before the emperor.

Decius spoke, "I am feeling merciful today, Christian. I will offer you an opportunity to save yourself. If you tell me where your church hides its actual treasure and sacrifice to the gods of Rome, I will let you go free."

Lawrence responded, "I cannot do as you ask. Let me instead offer you the opportunity to accept Christ Jesus and repent of your sins."

Decius didn't hesitate. "Restrain him on a gridiron! I want him slowly roasted to death!"

Lawrence was restrained, and a fire was lit.

The emperor watched for a time, then, when it was clear that Lawrence was nearing his end, Decius asked him, "Have you nothing to say, Christian?"

"Yes," replied Lawrence with a smile. "I am well done on this side, you should turn me over."

Emperor Decius dismissed his soldiers and stormed off in disgust, leaving the body of Lawrence to continue to roast until the fire died.

*   *   *

The following morning, Hippolytus recovered the deacon's body and took it to the Campus Veranus where many Christians were buried. There he laid Lawrence to rest so that Christians who wished to pay their respects could pray at the graveside.

Many people who encountered Lawrence during his final days were moved to conversion. One of those converts was a man named Hippolytus, formerly a Prefect of Rome.

St. Anthony's Chapel has relics from St. Lawrence of Rome on display in several cases around the chapel. During the three days granted by the emperor for St. Lawrence to gather together the treasures of the

Church, he sent a chalice back to his parents in Spain for safekeeping. Today, the chalice is on display in Valencia Cathedral. Some claim that this chalice is the famous Holy Grail used at the last supper. While this is unlikely, it is very likely that the chalice St. Lawrence sent to his parents is the chalice used by the early popes to celebrate Mass. St. Lawrence was martyred in 258 A.D. His feast day is August 10th. St. Lawrence of Rome has several patronages including the city of Rome, cooks, and firefighters. A somewhat different version of this story was recorded by WAOB Audio Theatre, and is available at their website under the title "The Treasures of the Church."

St. Vitus

In Strasbourg, the summer of 1518 had been unusually cold and wet. It was now July, and there were snow flurries in the air. The crops had largely failed, and starvation over the coming winter had become a real possibility for many. A pall hung over the city, and some people were now openly questioning whether God was punishing them for some offense, or worse, had abandoned them.

*　　*　　*

Frau Troffea was a fairly typical middle-aged woman. She was thin, with long grey hair, and she wore a stiff white apron over her ankle-length blue linen dress. Her stockings were wool, and her slit leather shoes were loose fitting, without laces.

Frau Troffea was tired, hungry, and afraid. The lines on her face, her tightly pressed lips, and her anxious eyes all conveyed a sense of hopelessness and despair. She was losing her faith.

Then, in a moment of anger at God, Frau Troffea did something extraordinary. She stepped out into the street, and there, amid the mud and the straw, the pigs and the geese, Frau Troffea began to dance. As she danced, others slowly joined in. By the end of the day, there were a dozen dancers; by the end of the week, there were forty.

The dancing may have simply been a reaction by people who were under great stress. It may have been an act of defiance against a God perceived as angry or absent, it may have been connected in some way to the efforts of the Protestant reformers then underway, or it may have been something truly sinister, truly demonic.

The dancers danced as if they were mad or possessed. They whirled and shook compulsively, unable to stop. They danced until they broke the bones in their feet and their shoes filled with blood. A few people even danced until their hearts failed and they died.

A number of physicians were consulted. They were divided in their opinions, and a number of treatments were tried, all to no avail. The guildhalls were opened, and the city hired musicians to play, in the hope that the dancers could simply be exhausted, but the dancing plague did not abate. It continued to spread like a fever. Each day, more and more people fell under its strange spell. By the first week of August, there were more than four hundred dancers.

The dancers tore at their clothes, they shouted curses against God, they spat, and they attacked spectators and passersby, until finally the citizens of Strasbourg decided upon a desperate plan.

On August 10th, all those who were still able-bodied assembled at the city center. They brought with them every wagon, every cart, and every draft animal that they could find. They restrained the dancers with ropes, bound them together, and loaded them onto the wagons and carts, or tied them down over the backs of horses and oxen. Then they pushed and pulled the dancers along the rutted road that led out of Strasbourg, as the dancers flailed and kicked against their restraints.

Then the rains came. The wind blew and the thunder rolled. Still, the strange procession continued to slowly wind its way up into the mountains of Alsace. For nearly a week the people of Strasbourg followed their priest through the mud, slipping and sliding up, up, up to their mountaintop destination.

*   *   *

Finally, the people of Strasbourg came to the shrine of St. Vitus.

There the priest said a short prayer. Then he addressed the crowd.

"My dear friends in Christ, when the Roman Emperor Diocletian issued his famous edict against the Christians, Roman soldiers swept through Lucania in southern Italy, putting many to death. St. Vitus was martyred, together with two members of his household. His relics have since been disbursed to many churches and shrines around Europe, which is what brings us to this place . . . "

*   *   *

The sick were brought before the shrine a few at a time. As they came forward, the priest pronounced a blessing over them, and their families prayed for the intercession of St. Vitus. As their families prayed, the strange compulsion left the dancers, and their minds were restored to them. They ceased to flail and kick. They ceased to spit and curse. Many fell into an exhausted sleep, and in this way, the strange case of the dancing sickness was finally brought to an end.

St. Vitus

St. Vitus grew up in Sicily. He may have been an actor or comedian. As an adult, he moved to the Roman province of Lucania in southern Italy. In 303 A.D., the Roman military swept through Lucania executing Christians on the order of Emperor Diocletion. In a matter of weeks, hundreds of Christians were put to death. St. Vitus is one of nine Lucanian martyrs that we know by name. He is consistently associated with two other Lucanian martyrs, Modestus and Crescentia, who were likely members of his household. Some traditions say Modestus was his tutor.

Vitus was venerated locally as a saint from the time of his death, and his grave immediately became a shrine and a place of pilgrimage for the Christians who survived the purge. His relics were later translated to Rome and then, in the ninth century, to a new church in northern Germany. There they were enshrined in the church as part of its dedication ceremony. Over the next three hundred years, small pieces of bone were gifted to churches and shrines around Europe. As a result, by the Middle Ages there were many churches and shrines dedicated to St. Vitus, and he became a very popular saint.

One such shrine to St. Vitus was located in the mountains outside of Strasbourg. The compulsive dancing event of 1518 ended only when the afflicted were taken before the shrine. The people of Strasbourg credited the end of the dancing sickness to the intercession of St. Vitus. Thereafter, it became a tradition to dance at his shrine on his feast day, a practice that continued for more than century.

St. Anthony's Chapel has relics from Saints Vitus, Modestus, and Crescentia on display at various locations around the chapel. St. Vitus Dance is an old name for epilepsy. St. Vitus is the patron saint of actors, comedians, dancers, and epileptics. His feast day is June 15th.

SAINTS PERPETUA AND FELICITY

Perpetua and her servant Felicity were under arrest, but Perpetua was a Roman citizen and an aristocrat, so they were afforded certain privileges. They were allowed to stay together, in a room with a window, and they were allowed visitors.

Perpetua was also allowed to keep a diary.

"What are you writing now?" asked Felicity.

"My most recent vision," replied Perpetua.

Felicity was well into her pregnancy. She shifted this way and that as she tried to find a comfortable position. It was hot, and sweat beaded on her dark skin. "What did you see?" she inquired.

Perpetua put down her stylus and took a moment to compose herself. Then she turned to Felicity and said, "Several days ago, I found myself thinking of Dinocrates."

"Your brother . . . the one who died as a child?"

"Yes," continued Perpetua. "I found myself thinking about poor little Dinocrates. That night, I experienced a vision. In the distance, across a stretch of desert, I saw a dark and gloomy cave, and I knew that it was full of suffering souls. Between the cave and me, there was a beautiful fountain. Dinocrates came out of the cave. I could see him, but I could not go to him. I could see a sore on his face. He was as I remembered him, suffering greatly from the cancer that took him at age seven. He went to the fountain, desperate for a drink, but the fountain was too high for him, and try as he might, he could not reach the water."

"What do you think it meant?" asked Felicity.

"That he is suffering," replied Perpetua. "But that is not the end of my story."

"No?"

"No," said Perpetua. "I realized that I should pray for him . . . so for the last several days, I have prayed for the repose of his soul, and I have now been given a second vision."

"You saw Dinocrates again," Felicity anticipated.

"Yes," said Perpetua. "But this time things were very different. I saw Dinocrates, and the sore on his face was well healed. He was happy, and ran about, playing as a child should. There was also a man, whom I took to be an angel. He stood next to the fountain and filled a goblet for Dinocrates whenever he wanted to drink. I knew then that Dinocrates would soon be delivered from his place of punishment."

"It will soon be our time to join him in heaven," said Felicity.

"Indeed, it will," replied Perpetua. "My father came earlier today. Our sentence has come down. We are to be torn apart by wild beasts."

Felicity looked out the window. Each afternoon, a crowd would gather outside of the prison, hoping for a glimpse of the two Christian women. People were starting to assemble.

Perpetua looked at Felicity's swollen belly and felt great sadness for her unborn child. Then she closed her eyes and thought of her own infant son, who, for love of Christ, she would never see again.

Saints Perpetua and Felicity

St. Perpetua was a Roman noblewoman who lived in Carthage, North Africa. She was a catechumen who was arrested with her brothers and her servant Felicity for failure to perform required pagan sacrifices. While in prison, Perpetua kept a diary. Her diary was combined with the prison diary of her catechist, Saturus, and the testimony of several witnesses, to create The Martyrdom of Perpetua and Felicity, shortly after her execution. She was initially sentenced to be torn apart by wild beasts. When the beasts did not cooperate, Perpetua was beheaded. She died in 203 A.D. Her diary provides important early evidence that the Jewish practice of praying for the dead (Orthodox Jews still pray for the dead) was continued by the earliest Christians, and was not a later corruption of the faith, as some have argued. Purgatory was there from the beginning. St. Anthony's Chapel has relics from Saints Perpetua and Felicity on display in various cases around the chapel. Their feast day is March 7th (March 6th prior to 1969). They are patrons for mothers, expectant mothers, and for Catalonia.

Pope St. Callixtus

It's August. The sun is shining brightly, and it's hot. Portus is busy. Dozens of ships are moored along the waterfront. Longshoremen are unloading cargo from around the empire: perfume from Arabia, precious stones from North Africa, tin from Britannia, and wine from Gaul. The streets are crowded with people speaking a dozen different languages, and the warehouses along the wharf smell of mold and exotic spices.

There is great wealth here, but there is also a seediness about the place. A block off the quay, rats scurry down the alleyways, and on every corner barkers call out to the sailors on leave, advertising the taverns, brothels, and gambling halls that are ubiquitous throughout the town.

Amid all this activity stands one man in particular. He is young, about twenty. He is short and stocky, with deep-set brown eyes, and tight curly black hair. He is a Christian. He is also a slave, though that is not apparent from his appearance. He is well fed. He is well dressed. His beard and nails are neatly trimmed.

He is also soaking wet . . . and in custody.

His name is Callixtus.

*   *   *

Gallus the slave catcher spoke. "He has been captured."

"Where?" asked Carpophorus.

"Portus," Gallus replied. "He had boarded a ship, but we were able to prevent the ship from leaving the harbor. He leapt over the side and tried to swim to shore. We pulled him out of the water."

"No money?" asked Carpophorus.

"No," replied Gallus.

"You know, I trusted him," Carpophorus said softly, as tears welled up in his eyes. "He was born a freeman. He's educated . . . knows how to keep books. I did not take him for an embezzler."

"You can discipline him as you like now," responded Gallus.

"No, I cannot," continued Carpophorus. "My creditors have opened an estate for the collection of my debts. Without the money Callixtus stole, I cannot pay them. I am afraid the matter is out of my hands. His fate will be determined by the magistrate, who will almost certainly send him to the mines."

*   *   *

Callixtus was in failing health. The mines were dark and hot. The air was stale and full of salt. His eyes watered, his lungs burned, and he had lost a great deal of weight.

The miners were given too little food and too little rest. As convicts, they were slowly worked to death. Callixtus had been here for nearly a year, and the hard labor and impoverished conditions were taking their inevitable toll.

*   *   *

Emperor Commodus was a cruel man, who lived out his

gladiatorial fantasies by fighting cripples and unarmed men in the arena. Narcissus was a wrestler. The emperor had recruited Narcissus to serve as his personal trainer, but he had developed another, more important, use for Narcissus. Narcissus was known for his discretion. He could keep a secret, and Emperor Commodus had secrets that needed keeping. Narcissus the wrestler now served as the emperor's confidential intermediary.

Narcissus arrived at the Villa Quintilii for a private meeting with the emperor. He was made to wait until Commodus returned from the baths. Then the two men went for a walk in the garden. The orange blossoms were in bloom, and the garden smelled of citrus.

The emperor's curly blond hair was still wet, and appeared almost golden in the early morning light. Narcissus found himself wondering whether the rumors were true; perhaps the emperor was illegitimate. He certainly looked nothing like his father, Marcus Aurelius.

At the fountain, the two men stopped.

"A response from Marcia?" Commodus asked.

"Yes, Caesar," replied Narcissus.

"And . . . ?"

"She consents to be your mistress, on one condition," said Narcissus.

"What does she want?" asked the emperor absentmindedly. "A villa, slaves, a stipend to support her after I have lost interest and moved on to another?"

"No, Caesar," replied the prefect. "Her request is most unusual. She consents to be your mistress provided you free the Christians consigned to the salt mines on Sardina."

Commodus furrowed his brow. "Why?" he asked.

"She would not explain herself. Apparently she has some sympathy for the Christians. I have heard a rumor that her brother may be one," said Narcissus.

Commodus paused for a moment, and then said, "Ah, she is the most beautiful woman of the age! It is only fitting that she should be mistress to the emperor! I will grant her request. Ask Prefect Perennis to draw up the order."

Then with a wave of his hand, the emperor dismissed Narcissus.

* * *

Callixtus found himself in Naples. His release from the salt mines had been completely unexpected, and, quite possibly, an accident. Callixtus had to wonder whether Emperor Commodus had realized that there were Christians toiling away in the mines for crimes unrelated to their religion. Had the emperor really intended to free an embezzler?

Callixtus reflected on the strange twists and turns his life had taken: freeman to slave, slave to convict, convict to freeman.

Callixtus was staying with a Christian family in Naples. They were caring for him while he recovered from his time in the mines. During this extended convalescence, he would have time to think about providence, mercy, forgiveness, and second chances.

* * *

Eight months had passed since his release from the mines,

and Callixtus was back in Rome. His eyes were still red. They watered constantly, and he struggled with a persistent cough, but he had put on some weight and his energy level was improving. The Church had now hired him to dig graves in the catacombs south of the city, and Callixtus was very grateful for the opportunity to live by simple, honest work.

As Callixtus tended to the Christian dead and reflected on his time in the mines, he developed a theology that emphasized God's mercy and the importance of forgiveness. Ideas that would find full expression a few years down the road, when, in yet another strange turn of events, Callixtus would become pope.

St. Anthony's Chapel has several relics from Pope St. Callixtus on display in various cases around the chapel. The story of Pope St. Callixtus is full of improbable twists and turns. Callixtus was deeply affected by his experiences as a slave and, later, as a convict. As pope, Callixtus emphasized the importance of God's mercy. He was the first pope to declare doctrinally that all properly confessed sins can be forgiven, allowing even adulterers and murders to return to the Church, a controversial position at the time. The catacombs where he worked as a gravedigger are still known today as the Catacombs of St. Callixtus. He died in 223 A.D. He is the patron saint of cemetery workers. His feast day October 14th.

St. Quentin

Eusebia led her companions deep into the swamp.
The night was dark. Torches flickered and lamps swayed.
At the edge of the light, shadows leapt and danced like devils, and
fog swirled into wispy phantoms that crept about among the trees.
The swamp was an unpleasant place during the day. At night, it
was downright spooky.

"Crooooooaak," went the frogs.

"Bzzzzzzz," went the flies and mosquitos.

"Hooooot," went an owl.

"GRRRRRREEEAHHOOOW," went *something* out in the darkness.

Eusebia was old and blind. She wore a woolen hooded cloak
over an ankle-length linen dress that gathered mud about the hem
as she made her way through the bog. The gold chain draped
across her forehead was the only indication that she came from the
Roman nobility. Many Roman nobles in Gaul were now Christian,
but Eusebia was particularly devout. She spent most of her time
in prayer.

Four days earlier, Eusebia had informed her family and servants that she had experienced a vision. Now her household and a
number of curious villagers found themselves following her into a
dark, steamy swamp late on a summer's night. They had come to
see if her vision had been true. A few believed, but most did not.

Two nervous servants stayed close to Eusebia to make sure she did not stumble, but they were not needed. Despite her blindness, Eusebia somehow made her way through the swamp without assistance.

This marshy lowland around the Somme River was said to be haunted, and it was certainly home to robbers and snakes. Everyone kept a watchful eye, mindful of the many dangers lurking in the darkness.

In time, Eusebia led everyone to a deep pool. The pool was clouded with peat, and it smelled of rotten eggs. Only a few sluggish eddies disturbed its otherwise calm surface.

"This is the place. Now we must wait," she announced in a hushed voice.

Everyone came forward and crowded together at the water's edge. By the light of their torches and lamps, they could see mist rising from the surface of the water and little ripples left by the passing of water bugs.

For a time, nothing happened. Then the rotten egg smell began to fade away. Soon the air was filled with a pleasant floral scent, spicy, and a bit earthy, like wild primrose.

Eusebia looked to her left and cocked her head, as if listening to someone that only she could hear.

"Now!" she shouted.

Just then, bubbles began to appear on the surface of the water. Only a few bubbles at first, but then more and more. The bubbles came faster, and faster, and faster, until the water seemed to boil. Suddenly, something surfaced. The thing bobbed wildly about amid the torrent of bubbles. Then the bubbles began to die down. After a few seconds, the last few bubbles popped away into the humid night. There were loud gasps and cries of astonishment as the onlookers discovered that the thing in the water was the body of a man. Eusebia's vision had been true! A few averted their eyes, but most could not look away.

The man was young, perhaps in his mid-twenties. His skin was white and shiny. As he floated about in the stagnant pool, his long, dark hair fanned out around his head like a halo, and water beaded on his body like drops of wax. His eyes were closed, his beard was neatly trimmed, and he wore a fine linen cloth about his waist.

Two men stepped forward to pull the body out of the water. As they did so, Eusebia received her sight! The experience took her by surprise, and she nearly lost her footing. For the first time in her life, Eusebia could see. She had to take a moment to compose herself. Then she smiled, and marveled at the faces of the people gathered around her. With tears of gratitude in her eyes, she spoke.

"Behold the body of Quentin, martyr for the faith!" she cried.

Her companions looked puzzled, and murmured among themselves for a long minute, until one of them finally spoke.

"Pardon mistress, but who is Quentin?" he asked.

Eusebia replied:

"My dear friends, nearly sixty years ago Emperor Diocletian persecuted the Christian Church. Quentin was a missionary who was arrested for his preaching. He escaped from Roman custody as he was being transported to Rheims for his trial. The soldiers who went after him killed him and threw his body into this foul marsh.

"Some days ago, an angel appeared to me to request that I perform an errand of mercy. Tonight, I followed the angel until he led us to this spot, and now we see that, by a special grace, Quentin's body has been miraculously preserved for us so that we may bury it according to our beliefs."

Quentin's body was carried to a nearby church. A few days later he was buried in the churchyard. People came from miles around to pray at his graveside. Some were healed, many more were converted, and in the little town of St. Quentin that grew up around his tomb, his story is still told to this day.

St. Anthony's Chapel has a relic from St. Quentin in case U to the right of the altar. Little is known about St. Quentin. He was a Roman citizen, possibly a senator or the son of a senator, who was arrested for preaching the gospel in Gaul. He escaped from Roman custody as he was being transported to Rhiems for his trial. He fled into a swampy area along the River Somme, where he was soon captured and executed on the spot. Later, his well-preserved body was recovered and given a proper burial. The town of St. Quentin, France grew up around his grave, which became a place of pilgrimage. This story is my retelling of an old legend about the discovery of his body. It was written in response to a challenge from WAOB Audio Theatre to write a children's story for Halloween. The recorded version is available online under the title "The Thing in the Swamp." St. Quentin is thought to have died in 287 A.D. He is invoked against cough, fever, and dropsy, and his feast day is October 31st.

ST. PETER

*"Amen, Amen, I say to you, when you were young, you dressed yourself,
and went where you pleased, but when you grow old, you will stretch out
your hands, and another will dress you, and lead you where you do not
want to go."*

— John 21:18

Prefect Agrippa was a wealthy man whose excess weight spoke to his many years of rich living. On this particular morning he was in his study, dressed in an expensive linen toga that he draped loosely over a crimson tunic embroidered with gold. His hair had thinned a bit, but it was still dark, and he was clean-shaven. It was his custom to attend to business in the morning, before making a visit to the baths, and then to share a leisurely meal with friends that would often last well into the night.

Despite his comfortable life, the prefect was troubled. It was late morning, and he was still at home, when a servant arrived to inform him that the emperor's friend Albinus was at the door, requesting to speak with him. Prefect Agrippa did not know Albinus well, but he knew that Albinus was not a visitor to ignore, so he asked his servant to show him in.

Albinus was angry. He had come to lodge a complaint.

"Agrippa! I must speak to you about the Christian, Peter!" he exclaimed.

"Ah, friend . . . " Agrippa started to reply.

"No! No!" Albinus interrupted. "My wife refuses to share my bed, and I have learned that it is on account of this Peter! She has fallen under his spell!"

Agrippa nodded in understanding, "I am dealing with the same trouble myself Albinus. I have four beautiful concubines who now deny me their favors. Each day around the noon hour they disappear, so yesterday I sent a servant to follow them discreetly. They went to a private house, where a crowd had gathered to listen to Peter proclaim his strange teachings."

"Why, then, have you not had him arrested?" asked Albinus.

"I am given to believe that Emperor Nero has plans to deal with him personally," replied the prefect.

"That should not deter you. I want the man executed! We need to restore order to our households. If Nero complains, I will speak to him on your behalf. If you do not move against this man, I will take matters into my own hands, and Nero will hear about your inaction!"

"Albinus . . . "

"Arrest him!"

*   *   *

That evening, Peter was preaching at the home of a man named Marcellus. Age had taken its toll. Peter's hair and beard were white, his back was stooped, and his legs were a bit bowed, but his eyes were still bright, and he was still on fire for Christ. He was a simple man, not well educated, not skilled in the art of public speaking, and yet he could hold an audience spellbound through his simple sincerity and personal witness.

That night, the people listened attentively as Peter told them of a cold morning long ago on the shore of the Sea of Tiberius.

"We had been fishing all night," he began. "We had little to show for our efforts. I was tired and ready for sleep, but Andrew wanted to try again in the shallows, so we cast our nets one final time. As we were drawing the nets back in, I noticed a figure standing on the shore, really just a silhouette against the dawn sky. I didn't recognize him, but he had built a little fire and seemed to waiting for us. As we drew closer, the man called out to us saying, 'Follow me, and I will make you fishers of men.' To this day, I cannot tell you why Andrew and I followed him, but we did. We left our boat and our nets behind."

As Peter was speaking, a woman pushed her way to the front of the group. She bowed her head and spoke. "Master, I am the wife of Albinus, and I have learned that he met with Prefect Agrippa this morning on your account. They are planning your arrest. Here, I have brought some of my husband's clothes for you to disguise yourself. My servant will accompany you to the Porta Capena. Once you are outside the walls, head south. I will send word ahead to Terracina. The brothers there will send someone to meet you on the road."

*   *   *

Peter fled south along the Appian Way. The sun was still below the horizon, but the sky was beginning to lighten. He was not far from the catacombs when he noticed a man approaching from the opposite direction, but it was not one of the brothers from

Terracina. It took Peter only a moment to recognize the man. There could be no mistake. It was Jesus, and he was dragging a heavy wooden cross toward the city.

"Where are you going Lord?" Peter asked.

"I am going to Rome, to be crucified again," replied Jesus.

Then Peter hung his head in shame. Jesus disappeared. Peter turned around, and started on his way back to the city.

*　　*　　*

Peter returned to the house of Marcellus, where he found many of the brothers and sisters still assembled. When they saw him, they gasped and cried out, "You are the witness; you must save yourself for the sake of the Church!"

"No friends," Peter replied. "I have met Jesus on the road, and he has reminded me of something he said long ago. It is time for me to stretch out my arms. I must bear this burden for the sake of my Lord."

As he was speaking, four soldiers burst into the house. They arrested him and stripped him of the fine clothing he was wearing. They dragged him naked through the streets to the Tullianum, the ancient prison on the Capitoline Hill. There they chained him to the base of column in the lower level of the dungeon, and left him to await execution at the pleasure of the emperor.

*　　*　　*

Peter sat naked on the cold stone floor of the prison. His long white hair hung down over his heavy brow. A single oil lamp, suspended on a chain, burned high overhead. The prison was dark, damp, and filthy. The air was humid and stale. It tasted of sweat and smelled of unwashed bodies.

Peter had long since lost track of time. How long had he been here? Weeks? Months? He really didn't know. Each day he would preach to anyone who would listen. Otherwise, he occupied himself with prayer. The men here were crammed tightly together. Fights were common, and sleep was rare, but Peter was far, far away, lost in his memories. He smiled as he remembered a day long ago when he had listened to Jesus, as they sat together near a warm spring at Caesarea Philippi.

Suddenly there was a commotion above. The grate opened, and Peter was summoned. Before he really understood what was happening, the iron shackle around his ankle had been released, and he had been pulled up through the hole in the ceiling. He found himself standing before two Roman guards, who dragged him blinking into the bright sunlight outside. The order had finally come. Emperor Nero had called for his execution.

Hundreds of brothers and sisters followed Peter as the guards led him to Nero's garden on the Vatican Hill. There, within view of the ancient obelisk that marked the turn in the circus race track, they brought forth a heavy wooden cross.

Peter spoke to his executioners. "My brothers, I beg you . . . I am not worthy to die in imitation of my Lord. Please, so my suffering may never be confused with His, crucify me upside down."

Peter's request amused the soldiers. They were not normally in the habit of taking requests from the condemned, but in this case, the stipes[3] had not been set, so it was no more work for them to

---

3   The stipes is the vertical beam of a cross used for crucifix-

crucify him one way or the other. They set him in place with ropes, then drove heavy metal spikes through his hands and feet. Once he was properly affixed, the soldiers leveraged the cross into place until the head of the old Galilean fisherman hung suspended a foot or so above the ground.

It wasn't long before Peter's heart began to race and his head began to pound. He began to sweat blood and, seeing his suffering, the brothers and sisters were outraged. They began to whisper among themselves.

"We are many."

"We could overpower the guards."

"We could rescue him and take him to a place of safety."

Peter guessed what they were discussing, and he spoke to the crowd. "My dear brothers and sisters in Christ! Please, stop your plotting! I accepted this cross long ago! Remember what Jesus taught . . . that we are to forgive and to love even those who hate us!"

As Peter spoke these words, the brothers and sisters found that their eyes were opened, and they saw two angels standing at Peter's side. Peter spoke to the crowd again.

"With the voice of the heart, I confess Jesus the Christ! Brothers and sisters, follow after Him, and you will find the things that no eye has seen and no ear has heard, and you will enter into His Kingdom!"

When Peter finished his address to the crowd, he closed his eyes and breathed his last. Marcellus was allowed to claim the body. He washed Peter with milk and wine. Then he anointed him

---

ion. The horizontal beam is called the patibulum.

with oil and herbs, before finally burying him nearby.

St. Anthony's Chapel has tiny bits of bone from the Apostle Peter displayed in several different reliquaries around the chapel. During World War II, a secret archeological investigation to find the tomb of St. Peter was conducted under St. Peter's Basilica at the Vatican. For those interested in further reading, the story of this investigation is told in The Bones of St. Peter *by John Evangelist Walsh, and in* St. Peter's Bones: How the Relics of the First Pope were Lost and Found . . . and Lost and Found Again *by Thomas Craughwell. St. Peter died between 65 A.D. and 67 A.D. His principal feast day is shared with St. Paul on June 29ᵗʰ. He has many patronages including fishermen and the papacy.*

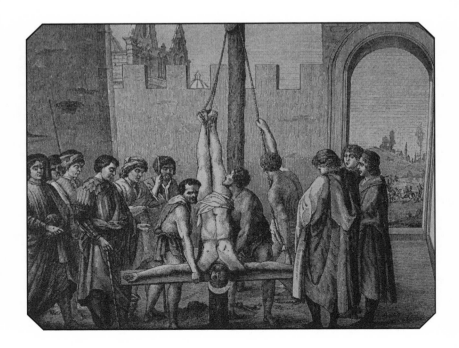

St. Onuphrius

I am Paphnutius the monk.

Some years ago, I left my monastery at Abydos to make a pilgrimage among the hermits who live in the old tombs and caves of the Egyptian desert. It was on this pilgrimage that I met Onuphrius the anchorite and came to learn something of the spirituality of the desert and the ways of providence.

The interior desert is harsh, and only the most committed religious live there. It is also strangely beautiful. The limestone outcroppings change color as the sun moves across the sky, passing from brown to yellow to red over the course of a single day. At night, the stars are brilliant, and only God could hope to count them.

In a cave not far from the Oasis Magna, I chanced upon my first hermit. When I found him, he was lying on a reed mat, and I thought at first that he must be sleeping, but when I touched his shoulder to announce my presence, I found that he was dead. I buried him as well as I could, and spent the night in his cave offering prayers for the repose of his soul.

The following morning, I resumed my journey. I continued southwest for several days, but I found no one else to call upon. My food and water began to run low. For a time, I was able to supplement my provisions with dates and wild herbs gathered near a small spring, but on the fifteenth day my provisions ran out.

I scanned the horizon, looking for palm trees or birds in the distance — anything that might indicate the presence of food and water. On the seventeenth day, my fear turned to resignation. I closed my eyes, and I began to pray.

As I prayed, I heard a voice. When I opened my eyes, I saw a strange beast standing before me. The beast was short, spindly, and impossibly hairy.

I was frightened. Instinctively, I scrambled up a nearby escarpment. As I did so, the beast called out to me. It said, "Come down to me, brother, for I too am a man of God."

I paused and took a second a look. The beast was indeed a man, though he was mostly beard and mane. About his waist, he wore a loose cloth made from coarsely sown palm fibers. What skin I could see was brown and leathery, and he was very old.

I must have been a sight myself, red, and blistered, and crazy from the heat.

The hairy old man came to me. He introduced himself as Onuphrius, and he offered me a stoppered gourd. The gourd contained water that he insisted I sip slowly.

We stayed in that place until evening. As the sun set, we started to walk. To me, the desert looked the same in all directions, an endless expanse of sand and rock that soon appeared chalky white by the light of a nearly full moon.

My new companion walked slowly for my benefit. It took more than an hour for us to make our way to his cave. The entrance was narrow and hard to see in the dark, but easy for him to find nonetheless, for just outside the cave there grew a single date palm that served as a convenient signpost.

The ground there was rocky, and it was getting cold when we

arrived. As hot as the desert is during the day, it is even colder at night.

I was exhausted. Once inside the cave I collapsed, while Onuphrius piled some scrub brush inside a circle of stones near the entrance and built a small fire. The fire burned with a spicy scent that I did not recognize, but it was pleasant, and helped to revive my spirits. The cave was small, barely large enough for two people. To one side, several reed mats and baskets were loosely piled on top of one another. To the other side, there were a few clay jars and bowls and two carved wooden cups. A tattered sheepskin hung from a peg.

Onuphrius produced two small cakes of salted bread, some oil, and a few herbs. He gave me one of the cakes. The bread was completely dry and very hard. I must have looked confused or uncertain, for Onuphrius smiled and explained that, in the desert, bread can be kept in this condition for several months. Then he poured a little water into a clay bowl, and showed me how to make the bread soft again by soaking it. He filled a second clay bowl with the oil and herbs, and then we dipped our bread and ate.

As we ate, we began to talk.

I spoke first, "Tell me, Onuphrius, how did you happen to find me? Why were you wandering so far from your cell so late in the day?"

Onuphrius replied, "I was not wandering. The angel sent me to find you."

"What angel?" I asked, but Onuphrius did not respond to my question.

Rather, he put some more some reeds on the fire and said, "As a young man, I studied law and rhetoric. I lived in the world and committed the sins of youth. However, I soon found wealth and pleasure to be empty pursuits. I met a Christian, and from him I learned the rudiments of the faith."

"He converted you?" I asked.

"My conversion took time," Onuphrius replied. "Gradually I came to see the world through new eyes. Eventually, I was no longer willing to make the ethical compromises required by my profession. I could no longer hold my tongue in front of the courtesans I once frequented. I could no longer bear to watch captive families torn apart and sold off in the slave markets."

His voice trailed off and, for a minute or two, he stared silently into the distance. Eventually, he turned to me with a smile and said, "I entered into a monastery near Antinoe."

"How long were you at the monastery?" I asked.

"Two or three years," he replied.

"But why did you leave?" I continued.

"In the monastery, I quickly fell into the rhythm of religious life. I found that I needed little food or sleep, and I learned the importance of prayer. I began to wonder how I could cultivate greater spiritual excellence in myself, how I could purge myself of my remaining attachments to the things of the world and cultivate greater discipline over my body. I sought to make my entire life a devotional act, a kind of living prayer."

"So it was then that you decided to become an ascetic?" I asked.

"No," he replied with a slow shake of his head. "I was led into the desert by an angel, and I realized that it was God's wish for me to serve in this way."

"In what way?" I asked. "How do you serve here, alone in the desert?"

"I pray for the world," Onuphrius replied. "In the desert, we turn inward. Through solitude and stillness, we quiet the senses to achieve ever greater union with God. We seek to never stop praying. It is the desert way."

"Tell me, Onuphrius, how long have you lived this life of prayer?"

"Sixty years," he replied.

I looked closely at Onuphrius. His face was brightly illuminated by the fire, but the rest of his body was lost in deep shadow. I noticed his eyes. They did indeed speak to his great age and to his many years in the desert.

"Have you lived alone all that time?"

"I am still visited by the angel," he replied. "And, from time to time, I meet a few Bedouin, mostly when they are out hunting with their falcons. I weave mats and baskets. If their camps are not too far away, I am sometimes able to trade with them for bread and oil."

"Tell me about the angel."

"The angel makes sure that I always have at least some bread or vegetables. He visits regularly, but rarely speaks. He often comes in the night. I will wake to find evidence of his visit in the morning. Mostly, he brings me the host."

"You are able to receive? Out here?"

"Yes," replied Onuphrius.

Onuphrius turned around and reached into the darkness beyond the light of the fire. When he turned back to face me, he held a small, shallow metal bowl with a fitted lit. He lifted the lid to reveal a small piece of dried flatbread. Then Onuphrius smiled broadly.

"You have reserved that for the Lord's Day?" I asked.

"Well no, not exactly," Onuphrius responded. "Out here in the desert, we never know when we will next have an opportunity to receive communion. It might be a long time, so it is a common practice for us to reserve a tiny bit of host. We expose it at night, and pray before it, and of course this way we always have an opportunity to receive at our time of dying."

An owl hooted somewhere in the distance. I looked out through the narrow cave entrance. Through a dark silhouette of palm leaves, I could see a few stars shining like polished silver against the night sky.

Onuphrius fell silent, and a change seemed to come over him. He looked up and, for a moment, he seemed to be listening to something that only he could hear.

"Onuphrius?" I said.

He looked at me and smiled a mostly toothless smile. Then he spoke. "Two days ago, the angel who led me into the desert all those years ago came to me and told me to go out and find you. You think that you have come here on a pilgrimage, to learn the ways of the desert, but that is only partly true. You have been brought here."

"For what purpose?" I asked.

"To bury me," he replied.

I should have been astonished at his remark, and yet I was not. Somehow, I knew the truth of it.

"Then perhaps I am meant to take your place?" I suggested.

"No," he said quietly. "You must return to the world, and deliver my message."

"Your message?" I asked.

"When you return, you must request a Mass in remembrance of me, and let the brothers know that any who offer incense at my memorial will be released from temptation and saved."

"And if a brother is too poor to offer incense?"

"Then let him offer food to the poor, or make some similar act of charity in my name," he responded. "Let the brothers know that if anyone recites the creed, or offers prayers to Almighty God in remembrance of me, then I will pray for his salvation, and stand as a witness in his favor on the Last Day."

Then Onuphrius bowed his head. He said a short prayer and closed his eyes. We sat together in silence as his breathing grew shallow. An hour later, he was dead.

After his passing, I became aware of the almost overpowering silence of the cave. The only sound was the crackling of the dying fire. I let it go out. As I waited for dawn, I found myself thinking about what life must have been like for the old hermit, alone here in his cave for so many years.

The ground was rocky, so when the sun rose, I covered Onuphrius with his lambskin and buried him as well as I could in a cleft in the rock under the shade of the date palm tree. Then I set off on the return journey to Abydos, so I could share his story with the world and arrange his memorial Mass.

I have often thought of Onuphrius since then, of how I was led into the desert to find him, of his deep spirituality, and of his promise to continue his work of prayer in heaven. I pray for his intercession, and I hope that, one day, I will see him again.

St. Onuphrius

     St. Anthony's Chapel has a relic from St. Onuphrius on display in case X along the left side of the chapel as you face the altar. We know about St. Onuphrius from the account of a monk named Paphnutius, who met him the night before he died. St. Onuphrius was one of the Desert Fathers. The Desert Fathers were early monks who went out into deserts of Egypt and the Holy Land to dedicate their lives to God. There they cultivated a unique form of spirituality that continues to influence Christian thought to this day. The practice of Eucharistic adoration likely originated with the Desert Fathers, who are known to have reserved consecrated hosts in their cells. WAOB Audio Theatre has recorded a slightly shorter version of this story under the title **The Hermit's Tale**. *The recording is available on their website. St. Onuphrius died sometime in the 4th Century. His feast day is June 12th.*

St. Catherine de Ricci

Catherine lit a single candle, adjusted the heavy iron chain that she wore wrapped around her neck and shoulders, then knelt before the crucifix. She began to pray and to reflect on Christ's passion. She was keenly aware that, while the sacrifice of the cross took place one time in history, there is also a sense in which that sacrifice is eternal and ongoing. Every new sin committed is another stripe, another painful wound that Jesus must endure in order to save those who would have a place in His kingdom. This troubled Catherine, and left her with an overpowering desire to relieve, in some small way, a little of Jesus' ongoing suffering by taking a tiny portion of it upon herself.

Catherine prayed until the world around her faded away. Darkness extended in all directions, and she found herself alone. For a moment, all was quiet. Then, in the distance, she could hear the shouts and curses of an angry crowd. A man spoke. "I find no guilt in him, but it is customary to release one prisoner to you at Passover. Would you have me release Barabas, or this King of the Jews?"

The crowd cried out, "Barabas! Barabas!"

Suddenly Jesus appeared before Catherine. He was standing next to a pillar and was accompanied by two soldiers. She watched as the soldiers stripped Jesus' to the waist and tied him to the pillar. Then they took turns scourging him with their lead-tipped whips. They counted as they went, keeping a deliberate and perfect rhythm until they reached the prescribed forty lashes. It was as if all of creation had been reduced down to Jesus, Catherine, and two Roman soldiers. The experience was incredibly intimate and, as the soldiers continued their terrible counting, Catherine found that she felt each lash upon her own back. As the whipcords cut and tore at His back, Catherine felt what Jesus felt. The pain was intense. Catherine fought to remain conscious, and for a moment she thought that she would die. Then she heard Jesus' voice in her head. He said simply, "You will not die," and while she still felt the pain, she also felt His overpowering love and compassion.

The vision faded, and the darkness returned. Catherine heard the shouting of the crowd. Again, the man spoke. "I am innocent of his blood. Do with him as you wish."

Jesus reappeared. This time he was surrounded by several soldiers. They mocked Him, punched Him, spat on Him, plucked His beard, and laughed as they called out, "Hail, King of the Jews!" Then they dressed Him in a scarlet robe, and pressed a crown of thorns down hard upon His head until little streams of blood ran down His face. The soldiers beat Him with a reed, and then placed it in His hand. Again, Catherine felt what Jesus felt. She experienced every blow, felt every pain, and she cried out when the thorns pierced her scalp.

The darkness returned. When Jesus next appeared, he was carrying his cross, and Catherine felt its heavy weight upon her shoulders. She could sense the presence of others, but they were present only as disembodied voices. She saw only Jesus.

When they came to Golgatha, two soldiers reappeared. Catherine watched in horror as the soldiers fixed the patibulum to the stipes, and drove long iron nails into His hands and feet. As they nailed Jesus to the cross, Catherine felt the pain of each hammer blow in her own hands and feet.

As the cross was hoisted into position, John, the beloved disciple; Mary, His Mother; Mary, the wife of Cleopas; and Mary Magdalene appeared at the foot of the cross. The soldiers faded away, and Catherine was left to watch with John and the women as Jesus spent His final hours dying an agonizing death. Again, she felt what he felt. As His breathing became labored, her breathing became labored. She tasted wine mixed with gall. Her heart began to race, and she felt a creeping coldness that began in her hands and feet, then moved slowly up her arms and legs into her body as His life slipped away.

Catherine cried out, "Oh, my Jesus! Oh, my Jesus!"

Jesus began to recite Psalm 22, "My God, my God, why have you abandoned me?" Then he cried out, "It is finished!" and Catherine felt the earth shake.

A soldier appeared and pierced Jesus' side with his lance to confirm that He was dead. Catherine felt an indescribable pain in her side and collapsed. Everything went black.

Catherine awoke on the floor of her cell. She saw that the candle had burned all the way down, and she realized that several hours had passed since the start of her ecstatic vision. She touched a finger to her face and found that she was bleeding from dozens of little wounds on her head. Her hands and feet were red and inflamed. There were long red welts across her back, and she felt a terrible pain deep in her side.

She called out for Sister Mary Magdalene, who came at once and helped her into bed.

St. Catherine de Ricci

St. Catherine de Ricci was born in Florence in 1522. She took the religious name Catherine, after her patron saint Catherine of Sienna, when she entered into the Convent of St. Vincent in Prato. Her prayers and devotions focused particularly on Christ's Passion.

Stigmata is the spontaneous formation of wounds or pain that correspond to the wounds inflicted upon Jesus during the course of his trial and execution. St. Francis of Assisi was the first known stigmatic, though the phenomenon probably occurred earlier. Some people think that the Apostle Paul may have received the stigmata. In his letters, Paul makes it clear that he suffered from some condition that others found off putting, and in his Letter to the Galatians, he says, "I bear upon my body the marks of Jesus."

In 1532, Catherine de Ricci experienced an ecstatic vision of the crucifixion, during which she received the stigmata. This experience was subsequently repeated every Thursday. Her stigmata did not always manifest in the same way. Sometimes she bled from her hands or her feet. Other times she bled from the head. Each time her wounds healed by Sunday morning.

She is known for great devotion to the Holy Souls in Purgatory, and is said to have appeared to St. Philip Neri in Rome while both were still living. She died in 1590 at the age of 67. Her feast day is February 2nd. She a patron of the sick. St. Anthony's Chapel has several relics from Catherine de Ricci on display in various cases around the chapel.

St. Theodore Stratelates (the General)

Earlier in the day, Emperor Licinius had arrived in Bythnia to great fanfare, but the social obligations had now been met, the honorary dinner had concluded, and the emperor found a few minutes to take General Theodore aside. While music and dancing continued in the hall, the emperor and his general retired to a private apartment.

"There can be only one," said Licinius.

"I thought you and Constantine had reconciled," replied Theodore.

"Temporarily," continued Licinius. "Constantine has his hands full with the Goths, as I do with the Sarmatians. Sooner or later, however, our conflict will resume. Rome can have only one emperor."

Theodore looked out a window at the night sky before drawing the curtain closed. There were oil lamps for light, but no fire, and the room was getting cold. He turned to Licinius.

"What do you need from me, my lord?" he asked.

Licinius paused, then in a serious voice he said, "Constantine has made himself a friend to the Christians. He has adopted their symbols as his own. Some say he has converted. Certainly his mother Helena has. I have to assume that in a fight for control of the empire, the Christians will support Constantine."

"I see," replied Theodore quietly, as he gathered his heavy red cloak about himself.

"I need to know that you are with me, Theodore. There are rumors . . . "

Theodore interrupted, "My lord, I will be only too happy to make the required sacrifice. I would however, like some time to adore the gods privately, in order to properly prepare myself."

"I am only here through tomorrow," said the emperor.

"Yes, Yes. I shall prepare myself tonight. If you will come to my villa in the morning, I will sacrifice to the gods, and demonstrate my loyalty to Rome and to you, my emperor."

"Very well, general," said Licinius. "I suggest you return to your guests."

*   *   *

General Theodore pulled a guard aside.

"Find ten men," Theodore whispered. "Then go to as many temples and shrines as you can in the next few hours. Gather together all the idols you can carry, and bring them to my villa. Set them up in my courtyard, next to the fountain. I will come to the courtyard at midnight."

The guard simply nodded his understanding before hurrying off to carry out his instructions.

General Theodore returned to his guests. He smiled, made polite goodbyes, and hurried home to his villa. He had work to do.

*   *   *

The sun was up, but it was still early when Emperor Licinius arrived at General Theodore's villa. A crowd had gathered outside the gate. A heavy plume of smoke was rising above the roofline from somewhere in the interior, and there was a sharp, persistent clanging sound as metal banged against metal.

Emperor Licinius didn't know what was happening, but he didn't like it. He began to shout orders from his litter. Soldiers began moving people aside, and slowly, the emperor and his entourage made their way through the gate and into the villa.

Licinius found General Theodore in the courtyard as expected, but the general was clearly not ready to offer the required sacrifice. He was stripped to the waist and covered with sweat. In one hand he held a hammer, and in the other a chisel. At his feet, there were little bits of gold and silver that had formerly been images of the gods of Rome. A crucible hung over a roaring fire nearby.

"General! Explain yourself," cried the emperor.

General Theodore laughed. "You said there were rumors . . . I expect so. I am a Christian, and I have destroyed your idols . . . broken them up, melted them down! I have spent the night casting them into little bits that I have handed out to the old, the poor, the hungry, and the sick."

Licinius folded his arms and pursed his lips. "I am disappointed, but not surprised. Seize him! Seventy stripes, front and back. Then crucify him."

General Theodore smiled as the guards led him away.

*   *   *

General Theodore was fit, but he was not a young man. He had barely survived the flogging. It was clear that he would not last long on the cross. Licinius watched as his general was stripped naked, nailed to the patibulum, fixed to the stipes, and hoisted into place. Then he retired for his afternoon meal.

When the emperor had finished eating, he dipped his fingers into a bowl of water and reached for a towel. Then he turned to one of his personal guards and spoke, "Go check on him. See if he is dead."

The guard returned to the place of execution. He looked around, but saw no sign of the soldiers who had been left to stand watch. The sun was high overhead now. The guard squinted and shielded his eyes with his hand. For a moment, he could see only the dark silhouette of the cross. Then, suddenly, he felt sick, and his knees went weak. There was no one on the cross. General Theodore was gone.

*   *   *

The following morning, Licinius was still fuming. He threw a chair across the room and thundered at his personal guards. "You couldn't carry out a simple execution! Where are your men? They must have helped him! Find him!"

As he roared in anger, the emperor was interrupted by a familiar voice.

"Your men do not need to search for me, emperor. I am here."

It was General Theodore, and there was something strange about him.

It took Emperor Licinius a minute to process what he was seeing. General Theodore had returned and surrendered himself. That was strange, but it was even more strange that the general

St. Theodore Stratelates (the General)

bore no signs of the devastating flogging he had received the day before. There were no wounds from the nails that had been driven into his hands and feet. In fact, the general was smiling, and he seemed exceedingly well. In another circumstance, the emperor might have asked if he had lost weight.

The emperor started to speak, but General Theodore anticipated his question.

"By the consolation of angels," Theodore stated flatly. "In any event, here I am. I am a Christian, and if the penalty for being a Christian is death, then it is my place to die. Carry out your sentence."

General Theodore was led back to the place of execution, and, in front of a large crowd, he was beheaded on the orders of Emperor Licinius.

St. Anthony's Chapel has the skull of St. Theodore Stratelates, also known as St. Theodore the General, on display in case X along the left side of the nave as you face the altar. After the Muslim capture of Damascus in 634 A.D., Muslim troops were garrisoned in a church dedicated to St. Theodore Stratelates. St. John of Damascus, who was a witness, records that the residents of the city found all the Muslim soldiers dead inside the church. Apparently, they had killed one another in a fit of madness, after one of them shot an arrow into an icon of St. Theodore and the icon began to bleed. St. Theodore is one of military saints. Like St. George, he is remembered in legend for slaying a dragon. He died in the Roman province of Bythnia, probably in 319 A.D. His feast day is February 8th. His principal patronage is for soldiers.

St. Vincent of Saragossa

The old widow was a Christian, but the persecution then raging throughout the empire had little affected her. She lived alone. She spent her days tending to her garden and looking after her chickens. On market day, she would walk into town to sell her basket of eggs. Otherwise, she kept mostly to herself and had few visitors.

Her cottage was a one-room, ramshackle affair that sat atop a rocky bluff overlooking a beautiful beach and the warm crystal-blue waters of the Mediterranean. Here, little desert streams became long waterfalls as they tumbled down out of the mountains to water several small oases where palm trees grew, and oxalis flowers bloomed throughout the year. In this personal Eden, the old widow carried on her simple but happy life.

Then one night, a strange thing happened. As the old widow readied herself for bed, there came a knock upon the door. She hesitated. "Who could possibly be calling at this hour?" she wondered. Nervously, she cracked opened the door. By the light of an oil lamp she saw Vincent, the priest.

Valerius was the local bishop. The bishop was a good man, but he was elderly and afflicted with tremors. He found it difficult to speak. Vincent had become his protégé. Everywhere that Bishop Valerius went, Vincent went also, and the elderly bishop was usually content to let Vincent do most of the talking.

Vincent was in his mid-twenties. He was tall and thin, with rich black hair that he treated with olive oil, causing it to curl up at the ends. He had a broad smile, and he was very well-liked among the Christians of Valentia.

The old widow was greatly surprised to see Vincent. She was surprised to see him because of the late hour, but she was even more surprised to see Vincent now, for as everyone throughout the province knew, Vincent had been dead for five days.

Vincent smiled. "Please, I beg of you, listen carefully," he said. Then he recounted the following tale.

*   *   *

On the orders of Emperor Diocletian, Bishop Valerius and I were taken into custody. We appeared together before Governor Dacian. When we refused to renounce our Christian faith, we were separated. Bishop Valerius was sent into exile, and I was thrown into prison. There I languished for some time. One night, I was taken from my cell, and again brought before the governor.

The governor is a cruel man. He looked at me with his hollow, sunken eyes and spoke. "You suffer needlessly, young Vincent. I have here one of your sacred scrolls."

With a long, bony finger he pointed to a scroll lying on a near-by table. Then he walked over to an ornate bronze brazier and began to warm his hands.

"You need only touch the scroll to the flame, and I will set you free." He said.

"Never!" I cried.

"Burn the scroll."

"No!"

"Burn the scroll."

"I confess Jesus Christ as Lord and Savior! The scroll on the table is an account of his public ministry, as remembered by people who knew Him and loved Him. You would do well to read it!"

"Take him back to his cell!" shouted Dacian.

For the next several days, I suffered the most horrible tortures. Then I was simply left to die from starvation. After I died, my body was taken outside the city and thrown into a bog.

*   *   *

Deputy Crispus was obese. He lived for food and wine. At the moment, his lips were glassy with duck fat and his fingers were sticky. Governor Dacian did not like Crispus, but he found Crispus useful. Crispus had a way of making problems go away, and Dacian had a problem. He stormed into the triclinium and interrupted Crispus at his table.

"Ah! Governor! Please join me!" cried Crispus.

"No. I don't have time. I need your assistance," replied Dacian.

"A glass of wine, at least," responded Crispus. He poured some wine for Governor Dacian, handed the wine to the governor, then clapped his hands to dismiss two young serving girls.

Crispus looked at the governor. "Excellency, how may I help you?" he asked.

"It's the Christian, Vincent," replied Dacian.

"What of him?" asked Crispus.

"I've had a report," continued Dacian. "The Christians follow the Jewish custom of burial."

"A strange cult, my lord . . . " Crispus said.

"A strange cult indeed!" shouted Dacian. "I don't understand . . . No matter. Crispus, after Vincent died, I ordered two of my guards to dispose of the body. I assumed that they would burn it, but I have learned that they took it outside of the city and threw it into the bog."

"Why is that a problem?" Crispus asked.

"Because I do not want the Christians to get hold of Vincent's body!" thundered Dacian. "I do not want them to be able to bury him according to their beliefs."

"Surely wild animals will solve that problem for you, if they have not done so already," said Crispus.

"That's just it," continued Dacian. "I know it sounds crazy, but two peat cutters stumbled across his body today, and it is being guarded by ravens."

"Guarded by ravens!" Crispus said with a laugh.

Governor Dacian stared Crispus into silence.

"I'm telling you, it's true! By some sorcery, his body is being preserved. It is only a matter of time before the Christians recover it. I want you to find it first and dispose of it permanently. No burial. No cremation. No site that might become a shrine. Find a couple of fisherman, and have them take it out into deep water and dump it in the sea."

Dacian drained his wine in one long gulp, then stormed out of the triclinium, leaving Crispus alone with his dainty bits of duck.

*   *   *

Crispus handed the fisherman their money, and the guards

handed Vincent's body over to them. The fishermen placed the corpse in a large linen sack. They tied the sack closed with one end of a sturdy rope. Then they looped the other end of the rope through a millstone and loaded the grisly cargo into their boat.

The sun was just coming up as the two fishermen put out to sea. The sea was a little rough, and the fisherman had to struggle against the waves. For more than an hour, they worked their way through the surf and out into the bay until they were more than a mile from shore. There, in deep water, well beyond the near shore currents and eddies, they dropped Vincent over the side. For a moment, the body in the sack bobbed on the surface as the two fishermen struggled to raise the millstone above the saxboard. Finally, with a heave, they threw the millstone over the side. It hit the water with a mighty splash, and the body of saintly Vincent was rapidly pulled down into the deep, dark water.

* * *

The following morning, the old widow rose early and went down to the shore to fulfill her promise to Vincent's ghost. She arrived as the tide was going out. As the sun appeared above the horizon, the retreating waves revealed the body of Vincent half-buried in the sand. The old widow laughed as she realized that, by Divine Providence, Dacian's efforts to prevent the Christians from burying their priest had become the very means by which his body had been recovered and would now be laid to rest.

St. Vincent of Saragossa

St. Anthony's Chapel has relics from St. Vincent of Saragossa on display in case V to the left of the altar. The place where St. Vincent's body was found is still known as Cape St. Vincent. He was secretly buried nearby. When the persecutions ended, a shrine was built over his grave. The story of St. Vincent is known from some very early sources, including a sermon by St. Augustine. During the time of Muslim rule in Spain, the Arab geographer Al-Idrisi noted that St. Vincent's shrine was constantly guarded by ravens. In 1173, Vincent's grave was opened, and his remains were taken to the Monastery of St. Vincent Outside the Walls in Lisbon. They have since been distributed to a number of churches and shrines around the world. St. Vincent is remembered for his eloquent defense of scripture. He died in 303 A.D. His feast day is January 22nd.

St. Roch of Montpellier

Gothard was rich man who guarded his possessions closely. One day, he became suspicious that someone was stealing food from his pantry. For the next several days he checked his stocks, and, sure enough, each day food went missing. Cured ham, dried sausages, bread, and wine all disappeared without a trace.

Gothard decided to lie in wait for the thief. He got up early one morning and slipped unnoticed into the pantry, where he hid himself carefully behind some flour barrels. A short time later, the door to pantry opened part way. Then, to Gothard's complete surprise, in came one of his prized hunting dogs, the black and white spaniel he called Ame. Sure enough, Ame pulled down a ring of dried seasoned pork and left the same way she had come.

Gothard found it surprising that Ame did not eat the food on the spot. He wondered if some clever person had trained her to steal, so he followed the dog, discretely and at a distance.

Ame left Gothard's estate proper, and entered into his hunting lands. She carried her prize of herbed pork deep into the woods until, at long last, she came to a young man seated under elm tree that grew along the bank of pretty little stream.

It was a beautiful fall day. The sun was shining. The air was full of birdsong, and the purling of the brook as the shallow water made its way down its rocky course. For a moment, Gothard almost forgot why he had come to this out-of-the-way place, but then he remembered his purpose.

"There is my thief!" he thought to himself, as he stepped out of the brush to confront the young man.

"Ho, there!" Gothard cried, but then he stopped. Something was wrong. He took a closer look and saw that the young man was desperately ill. He wore simple peasant clothing. His hair and beard had grown long and greasy. He was thin, covered with sores, and smelled of the grave.

"My name is Roch," said the young man, "And I have come here to die. At least that was my plan. As you see, I am nursed each day by this dog. She brings me food and she licks my sores. See, they have begun to heal."

Gothard spoke. "My name is Gothard, and I am lord of this estate. This is one of my prized hunting dogs. I call her Ame. Food has been disappearing from my larder. This morning, I hid in waiting to catch the thief. In came Ame, who took a ring of pork. I followed her here. You say she has been looking after you?"

"Yes," replied Roch.

"And how have you come to be dying along my game trail?" asked Gothard.

"I come from Montpellier," Roch began.

"Then you are a long way from home, my young friend," replied Gothard.

"I am indeed," continued Roch. "Two years ago, I set off from my home to make a pilgrimage to Rome. When I arrived in Italy, I met an old man on the road who urged me to turn back. He told me that a plague was raging in the towns to the south and that I should abandon my pilgrimage."

"He was right," said Gothard.

Roch managed a laugh, followed by a fit of coughing. Then he said, "Well, I did eventually abandon my pilgrimage, but I could not abandon the people in need. I continued on my way, and spent time caring for the sick in each town I visited. I was in Piacenza when I finally fell ill myself."

"And you crawled away from Piacenza to find a place to die?" asked Gothard.

"Just so!" replied Roch. "I hoped to find a place away from people, where I would present no threat to others and I could pass my final day or two in prayer, but as I lay dying your dog found me. She sniffed at me and whined. I urged her leave me to my fate. She left, but she returned a short time later with bread. Each day since, she has come to me with food or wine. She sits with me, and to my great surprise, I have started to recover."

Gothard was moved by Roch's tale, and he could not help but see the hand of providence in the unexpected actions of his dog. He helped Roch back to his villa and put him to bed. Gothard cared for Roch until he recovered, and the two men became good friends. Roch's compassionate example and simple faith caused Gothard to take a renewed interest in spiritual matters, after which he used his wealth to care for plague victims.

St. Anthony's Chapel has relics from St. Roch on display in several cases around the chapel. St. Roch reminds us that the merciful are blessed, for they shall be shown mercy. He is the patron saint of pilgrims and plague victims. His feast is celebrated on August 16th (August 17th by the Third Order Franciscans). He is thought to have died in 1369.

St. Nicholas of Myra

There was an old widower who had fallen on hard times. He lived with his three daughters in a simple cottage outside of Patara. The daughters were now old enough to marry, but the old widower had sold off most of the family's possessions and could no longer afford to pay their dowries. With no money or property to contract an honorable marriage, it was just a matter of time before the girls were forced into prostitution or slavery.

Then one night, shortly after the old man and his daughters had gone to bed, they heard a noise. Fearing that a prowler was about, the old man rose quickly and went to have a look outside. The moon was just a thin silver crescent, and the night was very dark. The old man searched as well as he could by the light of the stars, but he found nothing amiss. Half an hour later, he returned to his bed and fell into an uneasy sleep.

The following morning, the old man and his daughters discovered the source of the noise that they had heard in the night. On the floor of the cottage they found a small leather coin purse. Someone had thrown the coin purse through an open window as the family lay sleeping. Upon inspection, the coin purse was found to contain enough gold and silver to permit the oldest daughter to marry.

A few nights later, a second coin purse was thrown through the open window. The second coin purse also contained gold and silver, enough to permit the second daughter to marry.

The old man anticipated that a third coin purse might be forth-coming, and he determined to unmask his late-night benefactor. For the next several nights, he stayed awake as long as he could, but no one came to throw a coin purse through the window. The old man was ready to give up, when the youngest daughter asked him to stand watch one more night.

"Please, father, I too wish to marry. Somehow, I feel . . . I don't know, hopeful, that if you will stay awake again this night, then I will have my dowry, and we will know who to thank."

So the old man kept watch as his daughter had requested, and, sure enough, that very night another purse arrived. This time, however, the old man was ready. He stepped quickly outside, where he saw a shadowy figure lurking near the open window.

Hey! I wish to speak with you!" he called to the mysterious visitor, who took off running. The old man gave chase, and, to his own great surprise, he managed to catch his daughters' unknown benefactor in the garden, where he wrestled him to the ground amid rows of vegetables and olive trees.

The old man pulled the purse thrower to his feet and had a good look at him. He was young, not much more than a boy, and he had a very slight build. The old man thought he looked familiar. Then his eyes lit up with recognition. It was Nicholas! The bishop's nephew! The young orphan who served as lector at church!

"Nicholas . . . " he started.

Nicholas interrupted. Quoting from Matthew's Gospel, he said simply, "Do your giving in secret, then your Father who sees what is done in secret will reward you."

*   *   *

Nicholas had lost all track of time. He had no idea how many months he had languished in this filthy cell.

The guards usually turned a blind eye when the women brought him food. Still, he had lost a lot of weight, and he was plagued with a persistent cough and bouts of fever.

Bishop Nicholas was still young, but his hair had gone white, and his beard had grown long. He was tethered to an iron ring in the floor by a short length of chain. The chain ended in a heavy manacle that had rubbed his ankle raw.

The straw on the floor was crawling with bugs. There were no windows. A torch in a sconce on the wall provided the only light, when the guards remembered to light it. Even so, the dungeon was very dark and cold. In this place, men went mad and howled with despair.

Nicholas passed his waking hours in prayer. He preached when other prisoners would listen and offered everyone as much encouragement as he could.

Nicholas heard footsteps. Three or four people were descending the stairs. The door to the prison swung open, and daylight flooded his cell. For a moment, Nicholas couldn't see who had come to visit. He heard the rusty gate swing on its hinges.

"What is going on?" the bishop asked.

A man's voice replied, "Diocletian is dead."

*   *   *

The news spread fast, and all of Bari turned out for the occasion. Thousands of people lined the wharf where the merchant ship was moored. Thousands more packed every side street and alley running away from the waterfront back toward the center of town.

All were dressed in their finest clothes. Musicians played while clowns, jugglers, and mimes performed for excited children. Colorful flags hung from every window, and when the wind blew, the flags would snap to attention, pointing the way to the cathedral.

It was a beautiful spring day. The sun was shining. Planters, beds, and window boxes around the city were an eruption of color, full of chrysanthemums, roses, poppies, zinnias, and violets in bloom.

A priest emerged from the cargo hold of the merchant ship, and a cheer went up from the crowd. Two sailors followed, carrying a wooden chest. They were joined on the top deck by a number of nobles, church representatives, and other dignitaries. The priest offered a short prayer. Then he led the group down gangway onto the quayside.

The sailors, nobles, clergy, and other dignitaries fell in line behind the priest, who began to walk to the cathedral. The crowd followed, until they formed a procession nearly a mile long. With great fanfare, the procession wound its way slowly through the city until it arrived at the cathedral.

Many Christian shrines in Anatolia had recently been destroyed by the advancing Turkish army. Many precious relics had been lost forever, but that would not happen to the bones of St. Nicholas. St. Nicholas had now arrived at his new home, and the people of Bari nearly wept with joy.

*   *   *

Hans had been waiting anxiously for hours. "Is it time?" he asked.

"It's after midnight, I suppose we can try a sample," replied Ernst.

By the light of two hand-held lanterns, the men made their way down a winding flight of well-worn steps to the cellar. The cellar was deep and well insulated by thick stone walls. It was cold outside, but the temperature in the cellar varied little. The dirt floor was damp, and the air was a bit humid despite the season, but these conditions were not unusual and did not alarm the two brewers.

The winter casks were stacked on pallets against the far wall. The great oak barrels weighed more than 200lbs each when full, and Hans was grateful that they were already set on their sides.

Ernst wiped his large, meaty hands on his leather apron, then he grabbed a spigot and wooden mallet.

Hans spoke.

"Perhaps a final prayer?" he asked.

"Oh, very well," replied Ernst. "St. Nicholas, on this your feast day, we ask for your intercession to insure a fine beer. And please, don't let us make anyone sick!"

Hans laughed. Ernst struck a firm, decisive blow against one of the oak barrels. Then Hans produced two beautiful stoneware tankards elaborately decorated with hunting scenes as Ernst opened the spigot.

The beer was dark and rich, with a fine, creamy head. The two men smiled with delight. They quickly downed the draught and then happily refilled their steins.

Most of St. Nicholas' relics remain in the Cathedral of St. Nicholas in Bari, Italy, but small pieces of bone have found their way to several other churches and shrines around the world, including St. Anthony's Chapel. St. Nicholas grew up in the town of Patara, in what is today Turkey. His parents died in a plague when he was just a boy. Nicholas was raised by an uncle who was a monk. He inherited a considerable fortune, which he used to help the poor. Nicholas eventually became the Bishop of Myra. He spent time in prison during the persecution of Diocletian, and he is thought to have attended the Council of Nicaea. There are many colorful stories about St. Nicholas. The stories themselves are apocryphal, but they preserve the things that people remembered about him: his charity, his love of children, his concern for the poor, and his willingness to fight injustice. St. Nicholas is the model for Santa Claus. He died in 343 A.D., and his feast day is December 6th. Until about 150 years ago, the Feast of St. Nicholas was the day for gift giving and family celebrations. Christmas was for church. Traditionally, brewers tapped their kegs three times a year: summer, fall, and winter. In the medieval period, it became the tradition to tap the winter beers on the Feast of St. Nicholas. Brewers sought his intercession to ensure a good beer. St. Nicholas has many patronages including children and brewers.

St. Zita

Z ita grabbed the door handle.

"Wait just a minute, Zita. Where do you think are you going?" Asked Mrs. Fatinelli.

"To midnight Mass, mistress," replied Zita.

"Not dressed like that, you're not," said Mrs. Fatinelli.

"These are my best clothes," Zita protested. "It's Christmas Eve. You said I could go."

"Yes, yes. I meant that you need something warmer," said Mrs. Fatinelli.

Mrs. Fatinelli went to the hall closet. She took out a beautiful, heavy full-length wool cloak. It was bright red, with a high collar and polished ivory buttons.

"Here Zita. Take this," said Mrs. Fatinelli. "But please be careful. This is my best cloak. Mr. Fatinelli and I will be very cross if you return it with tears or lost buttons."

Zita smiled. "Thank you, mistress!" she exclaimed.

Zita draped Mrs. Fatinelli's fabulous cloak around herself and fastened the top button. The cloak was a bit long on her, but it was comfortable and warm. Then she opened the door and hurried down the front steps. The night was dark and unusually cold. The shops were all closed, and most of the merchants and their families were already in bed. Every window was covered in thick frost. Icicles hung from corner roof tiles, and there were a few snowflakes in the air.

The wooden heels of her shoes made a clop, clop, clopping sound as Zita walked down the uneven cobblestone street. Soon, she turned onto the Via San Frediano. As she did so, she heard the tower bells start to ring in the distance. She would have to hurry or she would be late for Mass.

Zita ran the rest of the way. As she approached the church, she could see warm light streaming out of the portico windows below the beautiful mosaic of Christ ascending into Heaven, and she could faintly hear the singing of the choir inside. She raced up the steps but, before she could enter the church, she nearly tripped over a poor beggar sitting in the doorway. He was dressed in threadbare rags and was shivering from the cold. The beggar didn't say anything to Zita, but he looked at her imploringly. Moved with compassion, Zita took off Mrs. Fatinelli's fine cloak and draped it over the desperate man.

"Here," she said. "This will keep you warm while I am inside, but it is not mine to give. I will have to have it back after Mass."

Zita went inside. She found a seat just as one of the servers rang the sacristy bell to signal the start of the Mass.

The Mass was magical. The choir sang beautifully. The statues and stained glass seemed to come alive in the flickering light of a hundred of candles, and the sweet smell of incense lingered in the air. There were four readings, including the Christmas story as recounted in Luke's Gospel, one of Zita's favorites.

When the Mass ended, Zita felt very happy and full of the Christmas spirit. All of her problems seemed far, far away. Then she stepped back out into the cold night, only to discover that the poor beggar had left and taken Mrs. Fatinelli's cloak with him. Zita's heart sank. She would have to tell Mrs. Fatinelli that her prized fleece mantel was gone.

The temperature had fallen, and the gentle snowflakes that had accompanied her on her way to Mass had now turned into angry squalls. As Zita hurried home, her face and hands went pale. Her dark, wavy hair clung to her face in long, wet strands, and her lips turned blue.

She crept quietly back into the house. The family and the other household servants were all fast asleep, but Zita had to stay up. She had been granted her request to go to midnight Mass, but she would now have to work through the night to bake the sweet breads. The family would expect them to be ready in the morning.

When Christmas morning arrived, the Fatinelli family came downstairs to find Zita just taking the sweet breads out of the oven. She was exhausted and covered with flour. With tears in her eyes, Zita presented herself to Mrs. Fatinelli to explain what had become of the expensive red cloak.

Just then, there was a knock at the front door. Mr. Fatinelli answered it. When he opened the door, he was surprised to find a poor beggar holding Mrs. Fatinelli's red cloak in his hand. The beggar simply smiled and handed the cloak to Mr. Fatinelli. Then, without a word, he turned and walked down the front steps. Suddenly, there was a strong gust of wind, and the silent beggar disappeared behind a curtain of windblown snow. A moment later, when the snow cleared, the beggar was gone.

Mr. Fatinelli rushed outside to search for the poor *mendicante*. At the bottom of the stairs, he looked this way and that. He ran out into the street shouting, "Hello! Hello!" but the only reply he received was the icy howl of the wind. Mr. Fatinelli was so stunned by the man's disappearance that, for a minute or two, he simply did not feel the cold, and he lost track of the passage of time.

"Pagano, get back in here this instant!" cried Mrs. Fatinelli. "You'll catch your death standing out there in your nightclothes!"

The sound of his wife's voice brought Mr. Fatinelli back to the present, and he realized that he was indeed standing in the snow in his nightshirt and stocking feet. He came back inside and sat down while one of the servants went to get hot water and a blanket.

As the color returned to Mr. Fatinelli's cheeks, Zita told everyone about her experience the night before. They listened and were amazed. For some time after Zita finished speaking, the family and servants discussed the matter, until finally Mr. Fatinelli declared, "I can see no other explanation. Surely, this man was no ordinary beggar, but an angel of God, who responded to Zita's compassion by visiting us this morning. What a wonderful gift we have received this Christmas!"

Soon, everyone in the little Tuscan town of Lucca had heard the story of Zita, the angel, and the cloak. To this day, the story is told every Christmas in that part of Italy, and the door to the Basilica of San Frediano where Zita met the poor beggar is still known as the angel's door.

St. Anthony's Chapel has a small piece of bone from St. Zita on display in case ZH toward the rear of the chapel, on the left side as you face the altar. Many saints exhibit an unusual resistance to decay after death. These saints are collectively referred to as the incorruptibles. St. Zita died in 1272. When her body was exhumed in 1580, it was found to be in-

corrupt. It has since mummified. Her mummified remains, minus a bit of bone here and there, are on display at the Basilica of San Frediano in Lucca, Italy. St. Zita is the patron saint of domestic workers and maids. Her feast day April 27th.

St. Philip Neri

It is shortly before midnight, May 26th 1595. The Church of Santa Maria in Vallicella is cool and quiet. Much of the church is lost in darkness, but here and there candles and oil lamps create pools of flickering light, and the smell of incense lingers in the air. The church is sparsely decorated, and the nave is filled with simple benches rather than pews. Not that long ago, Santa Maria in Vallicella was a ruin, but Oratorians have been restoring the church for the last few years.

Just in front of the high altar, under the watchful eye of two marble angels, five priests are gathered around the body of a man laid out on a table. The man has been dead for just about twenty-four hours. Word of his passing spread quickly, and large crowds of mourners have been streaming into the church all day. The crowds have only died down in the last hour or so, and the priests have finally been able to close the doors.

The man on the table is eighty years old. He is tall and very distinguished looking. His beard is neatly trimmed. His eyes are closed now, but in life they were crystal blue. He is dressed in priestly vestments, and, to be sure, he was a priest, but this was not always so. For the first fifteen years of his career, he resisted the call to holy orders.

There is a loud knock at side door.

"*Chi e?*" calls one of the priests.

"*I dottori,*" is the response.

The priest hurries over to the side door. He opens it to admit two doctors and their assistants. They are, of course, too late to be of any help to the dead man, but that is not why they have been summoned. No, the doctors have come, at the request of the Church, to perform an autopsy.

The sound of wooden heels crossing the marble floor resounds throughout the nave as the doctors and their assistants make their way over to the body on the table.

The assistants ready the instruments and open the man's vestments as the doctors make an examination of the body.

No one suspects foul play.

The Church is interested to know whether an autopsy can provide any evidence in support of a strange story that the dead man confided to two priests of his order.

* * *

The dead man came originally from Florence. His father was an attorney. He received an excellent education, and he was an excellent student. From a young age he felt called to a life of religious service, but he was always acutely aware of his own failings and he did not feel worthy of the priesthood.

As a young man he came to Rome. He took a job as a tutor, working for a family of modest means. They allowed him to live in their attic and provided him with one meal a day. In exchange, he educated their two sons. This arrangement left him free to wander the city for several hours each day. He spent much of his time simply talking to people. His kindness and good humor made him a very popular figure among the laborers and merchants of the eternal city, who came to know him well.

Then one night, one the eve of Pentecost, he resolved to keep a vigil in the catacombs of St. Sebastian. There among the dust of the martyrs, he prayed, "Lord, give me a heart big enough to do the work you want me to do." Whereupon he experienced an intense and overpowering sense of joy, and something like a tongue of fire entered into his body. Suddenly a great swelling appeared in his chest, and he collapsed to the ground overcome with emotion.

*   *   *

The autopsy is progressing, and the doctors have now discovered that the dead man does indeed have a strange distention on the left side of his chest. Upon further examination, they discover the cause. The ribs on the left side of the man's body are out of position, as if they have been pushed from the *inside*. The left fourth and fifth ribs are broken. They are simply floating freely in his chest, no longer attached to the sternum, an anatomical abnormality necessary to accommodate the man's heart, which proves to be twice the normal size.

The dead man was Philip Neri, founder of the Congregation of the Oratory and educator of young boys. He was known for his playfulness and sense of humor, often imposing silly penances on students who did not smile or laugh enough. He liked to play practical jokes, and he used humor to teach humility by, for example, wearing a cushion for a hat, following his maxim that a joyful heart is more easily perfected.

St. Anthony's Chapel has several relics from St. Philip Neri displayed in various cases around the chapel. He has several patronages including laughter, humor, and joy, as well as the city of Rome, and the United States Special Forces. His feast day is May 26th.

A Note on Sources

In writing these stories, I have consulted many sources, but relied primarily on the following: *The Miracles of St. Anthony of Padua* by Joseph Keller; *St. Anthony the Wonder-Worker of Padua* by Charles Stoddard Ward; *The Lives of St. Catherine of Ricci, of the Third Order of St. Dominic, St. Agnes of Montepulciano, B. Benvenuta of Bojan, and B. Catherine of Raconigi, of the Order of St. Dominic* by the Congregation of the Oratory of St. Philip Neri at Westminster; *WV's Golden Legend* by William Canton; *The Golden Legend* by Jacobus Vortagine; *Curious Questions in Art, History and Social Life, Volumes 1 and 2,* by S. H. Killikelly; *The Lives of the Saints* by Sabine Baring-Gould; *The Lives of the Saints* by Fr. Alban Butler (various editions); *The Little Pictorial Lives of the Saints* by The Benziger Brothers; *The Dictionary of Miracles* by E. Cobham Brewer; *The Book of Saints* by The Monks of Ramsgate; *Saints and Blesseds Whose Relics are in St. Anthony's Chapel* and *St. Anthony's Chapel in Most Holy Name of Jesus Parish* by Most Holy Name of Jesus Parish; the *Encyclopedia of Saints* by Matthew Bunson; and *The Catholic Encyclopedia* of 1913.

Made in the USA
Las Vegas, NV
14 June 2022